THE BEST OF
Lighting Design

THE BEST OF
Lighting Design

By Wanda Jankowski

PBC INTERNATIONAL, INC.
New York

Distributor to the book trade in the United States:

Rizzoli International Publications, Inc.
597 Fifth Avenue
New York, NY 10017

Distributor to the art trade in the United States:

Letraset USA
40 Eisenhower Drive
Paramus, NJ 07653

Distributor in Canada:

Letraset Canada Limited
555 Alden Road
Markham, Ontario L3R 3L5, Canada

Distributed throughout the rest of the world by:

Hearst Books International
1790 Broadway
New York, NY 10019

Library of Congress Cataloging in Publication Data

Jankowski, Wanda.
    The best of lighting design.

    Includes index.
    1. Lighting, Architectural and decorative.
2. Interior decoration. I. Title
NK2115.5.L5J34   1987   729'.28   87-4138
ISBN 0-86636-017-4

Color separations, printing and binding by
Toppan Printing Co. (H.K.) Ltd.

PRINTED IN HONG KONG
10 9 8 7 6 5 4 3 2 1

ACKNOWLEDGEMENTS

Thanks to all the designers and architects, and their staffs, who submitted projects for publication, regardless of whether they were published or not, for taking the time and effort to share their ideas with others, and for the enthusiasm they showed for this book. Thanks also to all the companies who submitted products—again, whether or not they were published—for responding to the call for information in a limited time frame.

My grateful appreciation goes to the public relations professionals who provided information on the organizations and the awards programs they represent: Ann Hardeman, Hardeman Marketing Communications, on behalf of the International Association of Lighting Designers; James H. Jensen, General Electric Company; and Len Lirtzman, The Hanlen Organization, on behalf of Halo Lighting. Thank you, Joanne Lindsley, for your help in getting this book underway.

My personal thanks to Abe Feder for his constant and unrelenting ability to come up with valuable new lighting ideas and insights and for taking the time to share many of them with me over the last 10 years.

If not for two professionals who are not now in the lighting field, I would not have written this book: the first was my editorial mentor, a former Editor of LIGHTING DESIGN + APPLICATION (LD+A) and my boss, who embodied then—as he does now—everything creative, professional and fine in an editor—Charles W. Beardsley; and second, Frank M. Coda, who appointed me Editor of LD+A, and inspired loyalty in his staff because he gave it in return. Thank you both. Finally, I wish to thank all the professionals at PBC International, Inc., who worked hard, well and pleasantly to produce this book.

—**Wanda P. Jankowski**

STAFF

Publisher	**Herb Taylor**
Project Director	**Cora Sibal Taylor**
Executive Editor	**Virginia Christensen**
Editor	**Joanne Bolnick**
Art Director	**Richard Liu**
Art/Prod. Coordinator	**Jeanette Forman**
Artist	**Daniel Kouw**

CONTENTS

FOREWORD

by Abe H. Feder

During my sophomore year at Carnegie Mellon, I was lighting the play "The Tidings of Mary." The last scene of the show featured a view of a mountain in the distance with a convent on top. We were fussing with it, trying to get a sense of the afternoon sun coming across this flat piece of scenery, which was really papier mache raised and indented to appear like rocks and the mountain. We spotlighted it, glowed it, tinted it, all to no avail.

Later that Saturday afternoon, I decided to come back to the theater alone and deal with it. I switched on the stage lights and noticed near the right side of the orchestra a girl practicing on the organ. I went to the middle of the theater aisle and looked at the mountainscape. The girl stopped playing, also looked at it and said, "That's not it." I asked, "What's not it?" She said, "I was born in California, near the mountains, and we never saw any sun washing evenly across the rocks. We saw streaks of sunlight, because of the indentations on the mountains—and that's not it."

I didn't show any enthusiasm. I just went up, focused some lights across the scenery and streaked it. When I got off the ladder, she said, "That's better, but the streaks aren't thin enough."

I didn't have any filter or shield that would thin the rays, so I scrounged up some cardboard and put that in the color frames on the spotlights. It thinned the streaks, and now she said, "You've got it!" I looked, and sure enough, the mountainscape seemed like it was 20 miles away with shafts of sun cutting across the rocks.

What's the lesson learned from this? There are several. Each has to do with what, I believe, makes a lighting designer.

First, unless you have the gift of visual awareness and memory, you shouldn't be a lighting designer. All the books published on lighting, calculations, the invented formats and grids, the reportage, all the assembly of minds who claim that this or that is the standard practice mean nothing if you do not observe what is around you, and cannot visualize how light affects everything you see.

When you conceptualize a design, do you really picture in your mind what the finished space will look like? Can you mentally frame it three-dimensionally? Some engineers will say, "That's not possible." They will produce calculations from fixture companies and copy one lighting layout from another. These engineers haven't the foggiest idea of what the installation could look like unless it's a copy of something that was done before. They lack the gift of visualization.

The other part of this ability to visualize light and space is a color memory. Red, green and blue are the three colors that make up white. Thousands of cones for each color exist in your eyes, those incredible instruments of vision. If you don't possess a sense of the relationship of color to what you see, you are better off being a gadget salesman, where a sense of color doesn't matter.

Understanding how light and color affect emotion is also a significant factor in being a good lighting designer. The theater taught me this, and it would probably benefit all designers to experience lighting for the theater and get a feel for it.

Henrik Ibsen's play, "Ghosts," was performed years ago by one of the greatest actresses of her day, Alla Nazimova. The last scene of the play takes place between a mother and her son in the living room of their home. On the right is a large bay window and beyond it can be seen the fjords of Norway. The mother is sitting at a table on which sits a lamp with a lighted glass bowl top. The son is seated on the couch. For a moment, there is a sense of warmth in the room, emphasized by the concentration of warmly colored light around the lamp. Then the mother speaks of the shocking fact that through the sins of his father, the son has been cursed with the disease of syphilis. Anguish is seen in the face of the mother as she turns off the lamp. In the few moments before she walks off stage, the glow disappears, and the room instantaneously changes. The gray light coming through the window sweeps across the room and echoes the hopelessness of the boy and the dreariness of the mother, transforming her face into a mask of death. It was first light and color that reflected and emphasized the glow of life in the mother, and then the gray, bleak light of dusk that reflected the coldness of death in her face.

This brings us to another consideration. The good designer has a gift of visualization, which includes an understanding of light's effect on people as well as on space. He also must have an appropriate attitude towards the tools with which he works.

If you want to write music for a 70-piece orchestra, you have to know what a bassoon, a fiddle and a horn sound like, or you're not going to write music. It will have no meaning if it can't be played. Like the composer, a lighting designer must be familiar with the tools of the trade.

The tragedy of mechanical technique, however, is that there is no critical view of the limitations of the equipment. Engineering schools treat as rote the mechanics of lamps, transformers, etc., as if it were some immutable testament written in stone. To have a critical view of limitations is to question: "Can't this be better?"

I vividly remember a man named Clarence Birdseye who walked into my office in the 1930's, when I was in charge of the lighting for all the Federal Theatre productions, and showed me a little reflector lamp. I asked, "Can't you make it bigger?" and found myself experimenting in my lab with some of Birdseye's fellows.

Well, we put together the first R-40 reflector lamp. We burned it. It was fabulous. I looked at them all and said, "Tell me, did anybody ever do this before?" Birdseye said, "No." So I broke the lamp. I thought they'd all have conniptions. I said, "Clarence, this is not fun and games. Test it again." The result was the birth of the first R-40 lamp.

I had in my equipment room striplights made from sheet metal about eight feet long with nine compartments. Before the invention of the R-40 lamp, these compartments would have held 500-watt A lamps, but the limited projectability of the light from them was inadequate for the purpose I had in mind. By replacing nine 500-watt A lamps with the 300-watt R-40 lamps, I had the equivalent of nine spotlights in one of those strips that projected down to the stage from 24 feet in the air. Given our limited knowledge of lamps at the time, it seemed like a miracle had taken place.

I feel the lighting evolution in our country has been primitive. But it's an ongoing evolution of which the designer should be conscious. Assume no complacency.

Though sources and fixtures have changed and developed, we're still in the "bottle/bulb age" of light sources. Soon there will be lasers, fiber optics, other forms of creating lighting energy and systems which will permit the designer a different palette of color, brilliance and tools with which to work.

Tools change. The good designer should be contributing to that change and not be victimized by the manufacturer. The manufacturer has to endow the product with capabilities; sometimes, however, what is stated in a catalog may not be accurate or complete. Always see how a lamp works first hand; test it yourself. And don't say, "This equipment is all I've got. I must design around it." Make the equipment work for you.

This leads to yet another consideration in what makes a good designer, and that is responsibility—to himself or herself, and to the client. In the 12th and 13th centuries, Italian painters operated ateliers. Young apprentices filled in the canvasses, roughing in patches of line and color for the masters. In the final analysis, however, the finished masterpiece was the vision of the art master himself—Titian, Tintoretto, or others.

You may have confreres, but eventually the design opinion has to be yours, and there's something dictatorial in that final opinion. There can only be one final choice—and chooser—of that design vision. It is yours.

Lighting is the art of revealment. What do you reveal? More often than not, when a client comes to an architect or designer, he has an idea of what he wants done. If he could do it himself, he would have done it. The lighting designer's responsibility is to create a vision—using his gift of visual awareness and memory, his experiences, conditioning and background—which will reveal as fully as possible the client's intent. The lighting designer should not superimpose his or her talent on that of others. He or she reveals that which is the design intent of others.

Finally, I would like to summarize how that enlightening incident in my youth at Carnegie Mellon illustrates what I have come to believe makes a lighting designer:

1. *Visual awareness and memory.* I transformed in my mind's eye that girl's verbal description of a mountainscape (since I had never seen one) into a three-dimensional vision of what I wanted that lumpy mass of papier mache to look like. That vision had to include intensity, color and the emotional effect it would have on the audience.

2. *Consciousness of product limitations.* I was stubborn enough not to settle for less because there was no product at hand that could thin the streaks of light. I modified materials to fit the concept.

3. *The designer's responsibility to himself or herself.* I came back to the theater alone to deal with the mountainscape problem. Unless I got it straight in my head—unless I had a vision—working with the assistants and electricians would have been a waste of time. And I didn't stop "fussing" until I achieved in actuality what I envisioned.

4. *Responsibility to the client.* The lighting design revealed the intent of the playwright. It did not call undue attention to itself. It worked as a coherent light "part" designed in harmony with the "whole."

In closing, I would like to leave this thought: As future societies invent and experience new forms of living environments—whether they be underground or in outer space—the tools, palette and methods of the lighting designer will evolve and adapt to them. However, the basic principles of lighting design—and what makes a lighting designer—will never change.

Abe Feder was the first independent lighting designer in both the theatrical and the architectural worlds. His firm, "Lighting By Feder," is located in New York City.

His Broadway credits are legion and include "My Fair Lady," and "Camelot." His architectural credits range from airports and geodesic domes, to miniature fountains and pocket-sized apartments. They include the United Nations in New York, Philharmonic Hall at Lincoln Center, Roosevelt Raceway, Buckminster Fuller's first geodesic dome, San Francisco Civic Auditorium, the terminal plaza of the Kennedy International Airport, Harvard Law School, the Minskoff Theatre on Broadway, eighteen of the Wickes Furniture Showrooms, the Kennedy Center for the Performing Arts in Washington, D.C., and the Rockefeller Center Plaza and Facade, the RCA Building, the Atlas Sculpture, and the International Building lobby in New York. He is responsible for many bulb and fixture developments which are now catalog standards.

Abe Feder was the first President of the International Association of Lighting Designers (IALD) and is an IALD Fellow, as well as a Fellow of the Illuminating Engineering Society of North America (IESNA).

INTRODUCTION

The projects collected in this book, except two, have received awards from the following lighting programs and competitions over the past five years:

Lighting Design Awards Program, sponsored by the International Association of Lighting Designers (IALD)

International Illumination Design Awards Program, sponsored by the Illuminating Engineering Society (IES) of North America

Edison Award, sponsored by the General Electric Company

Halo/SPI National Lighting Competition, sponsored by Halo Lighting and held under the auspices of the American Society of Interior Designers (ASID)

The main criterion for inclusion in this book was that the projects be top, or near-top award recipients in a lighting awards program or competition. Selection was not based on my personal taste but on the judgment of the many professionals drawn from the lighting, interior design and architecture communities who served as judges on the awards panels during the past five years.

One of the two exceptions mentioned above is the Rockefeller Center project, which received the 1986 Albert S. Bard Award for Excellence in Architecture and Urban Design from the City Club of New York. The award, usually presented to an architect, was given for the first time in its 24-year history to a lighting designer.

The second exception is the Statue of Liberty. It was completed in July 1986, too recently to have garnered any awards. It is included here because of its historic and national importance and because of the deft use of the latest technology to bring the designer's vision into reality.

Though this book contains a fine and varied sampling of the best of lighting design, it is not intended to be all-inclusive. Not all projects which have won awards in the above-mentioned programs in the five-year period are included here. Some are omitted because of time and schedule restrictions, others because of photographic limitations. In addition, not all outstanding lighting designers are represented in this book. There are fine designers who choose not to enter awards programs; others may have won awards in time periods or for projects not covered here.

The projects included in this book use a variety of light sources—from the pure beam of a laser, to the multi-faceted, complex array of sources integrated in a disco. Several styles are represented—from the decorative, refurbished chandeliers in a hotel lobby, to the angled shafts of light from concealed fixtures that draw attention to the altar of a church; from inconspicuous track lights in blacked-out ceilings used to highlight merchandise, to indirect fixtures in banks and offices that enhance architectural coffers.

Projects are featured which use currently available products—streamlined sconces and portable lamps, and simple, recessed downlights in a high-quality residence. Others are presented which use fixtures and sources that were custom designed—the slim line lamps for the exterior accenting of a shopping center, and new metal halide lamps which produce the desired color rendering of a statue's green patina. Daylighting applications are also included—active and passive solar systems that transmit light below the earth's surface, and mirror systems that transmit daylight into a New Mexico residence.

Installations with space and budget limitations are presented—a New York restaurant, a fashion showroom, a redesigned yacht. Also featured are large-scale, large-budget projects—a laser-filled condominium, a soaring Manhattan skyscraper.

Each of these projects displays the sensitivity of its creators to light as a design medium. They allowed light to contribute its own qualities and beauty to a space, while integrating it with the architecture and interior design.

Though the emphasis in this book is on the visual beauty and enhancement of the environment, engineering elements, calculations, measurements for beam angles and fixture positioning also were very much a part of the design of these projects. Practical requirements had to be satisfied in order for these installations to function successfully: Can maintenance be well-handled by the owner or the staff? Is the lighting energy-efficient and cost effective? Can the equipment be easily repaired or replaced? Can the owner afford to operate the system?

Because the designer's vision cannot be translated into reality without the use of wires, tubes, gases, glass, plastic and metals that make up lighting system equipment and its accessories, a chapter on new products is also included. The business of lighting and the kinds and costs of products are as much a part of the melting pot from which successful design ideas spring as the artistic and engineering considerations.

We hope you will find this book to be a valuable resource for design ideas, a compendium of concrete examples of techniques for creating lighting effects, and a visual embodiment of what results from an effective use of the qualities of a good lighting designer. As Mr. Feder explains in the "Foreword": a successful designer must have visual awareness and memory, consciousness of product limitations, and a sense of responsibility to his or her own design vision as well as to the client's needs and ideas.

—**Wanda P. Jankowski**

CHAPTER 1

BANKS AND CORPORATE OFFICES

Several years ago, in the midst of the energy crisis, a great deal of experimenting and designing with high-intensity discharge sources—metal halide, high pressure sodium, and combinations of these—was carried on in office environments in an effort to keep energy consumption and costs down. Though high-intensity discharge sources are still used today (the Calcasieu Marine National Bank featured here employs custom-designed metal halide uplight luminaires), fluorescent is still undoubtedly the most popular light source for use in offices. Fluorescent strips and furniture-mounted fixtures are used in the Calcasieu Bank, and custom-designed pendant-mounted luminaires are installed in both the Fidelity and Wells Fargo Banks.

Comfort and productivity in work areas go hand in hand. Interior design and architecture details that make a pleasant work environment can be enhanced significantly with the proper illumination. Some examples are:

1. Original fixtures and architectural details in renovated buildings may have a beauty and charm worth preserving. In the Fidelity Bank renovation, handsome, white glass hemispherical fixtures once used in elevator lobbies were cleaned. The lamps were replaced, and they are now being used in other areas of the bank.

2. Some companies add color and interest to the office spaces through the addition of artwork—paintings, framed posters and drawings, and sculptures. Artwork selected for display at the Wells Fargo Bank is illuminated brightly enough by recessed incandescent downlights to be seen and appreciated, but not enough to distract employees from their work tasks.

3. Plantings lend warmth to lobbies, reception and work areas. The trees and plants at Calcasieu Bank are lighted by lamps in framing projectors at 45 degree angles to create the impression that sunlight is shining through the leaves.

All those elements reflect a positive image for the company as well as create a pleasant atmosphere for the staff. In a couple of instances in this chapter, a positive image is created for the company through the view of the interior lighting from the outside. The Aetna Corporate Education Training Center glows at night and stands out in the Hartford, CT, landscape.

In many countries, cultural elements can add to the corporate identity as well as to the interest of the design of the space. At the Dae Han Insurance Co., Ltd., in Seoul, Korea, the chandeliers are modeled on the famous crown of the Shiragi Dynasty.

Many times, the decor of multi-purpose rooms cannot be changed to adapt to varied functions—large or small meetings, banquets, or special theatrical events. The lighting system, however, can create the necessary changes in mood. In the Lutheran Brotherhood Building's congregational facility, a theatrical lighting system with multiplex controlled dimming is installed in addition to an incandescent system. In the auditorium of the Dae-Han Insurance Co., direct and indirect lamps can be changed in intensity and color, and chandeliers can be raised or lowered via motorized lifts.

It is interesting to note the lack of award-winning projects that deal with visual display terminals. One can only guess that this is either because no outstanding solutions have been submitted for the glare problems on the screens, or that solutions for those problems involve much more than the lighting system alone can achieve.

Wells Fargo Bank

Lighting Designer: Jules G. Horton, Horton Lees Lighting Design, Inc., New York, NY
Interior Designer: Gensler and Associates/Architects
Photographer: Toshi Yoshimi, Toshi Yoshimi Photography
Project Location: Los Angeles, CA
Award: 1983 IALD Honorable Mention

The Southern California headquarters of Wells Fargo, the oldest bank in the West, consists of a branch bank, history museum, administrative offices and executive offices located in a downtown Los Angeles highrise. Displayed throughout the headquarters are approximately 300 works of Western art, by artists past and present, which symbolize the bank's past, present and future commitment to the West and its development.

Artworks displayed in a corporate space serve a different purpose than those exhibited in a museum. This difference is reflected in the lighting designed to reveal them. In a museum, intense focal points of light bring attention to artifacts, so details can be examined, studied and appreciated by viewers who come to the museum for that purpose. Artwork in offices, however, enhances the environment for both staff and visitor, but is not meant to distract from the performance of work tasks or the conducting of business.

Much of the artwork at Wells Fargo Bank is illuminated softly and subtly by low-voltage incandescent downlights, which highlight just enough to render clearly the colors and details, but not enough to attract special attention. In some areas, general illumination is sufficient for artwork. For example, a Bill Schenck mural behind a teller line is highlighted by a continuous row of wallwashers, a Farnsworth mural has adequate general illumination, and Tom Van Sant papier mache birds, suspended from the ceiling, are complemented by incandescent accents. Of significant importance to the success of the lighting design was the fact that the size, location and generic form of each piece of art was established early so lighting could be planned specifically for each piece before installation.

The same type of lighting is used on the planters. Visitors receive the impression that plants are gently bathed in sunlight and are unaware that illumination is from a planned artificial source.

In the branch bank and executive office floors, a pattern of rectangular recessed architectural coffers runs throughout the high ceiling. Indirect, custom-designed pendant-mounted fluorescent troffers are neatly suspended from the ceiling to provide general illumination. Most are 5 feet by 5 feet; some are 6 feet by 6 feet and larger, depending upon the size of the troffer. The light-colored coffer and clean line of the fixture contribute to the illusion that the fixture is lightweight. In some conference rooms, the indirect fixture is used with a direct component as well.

Tri-phosphor fluorescent lamps are installed in the troffers to provide a full spectrum of color rendering. Though they are more expensive than standard fluorescent lamps, they are as energy-efficient and long-lived. The cost is justified by the improved quality of the light produced.

Several steps were taken long before installation to insure the success of the fixture. Computer printouts were obtained indicating brightness levels produced at workstations by the fixtures and ceiling brightness patterns. Later, a complete mock-up of one ceiling coffer and fixture, with finishes, was fully tested and approved before installation was carried forward.

The offices on the administrative floors are illuminated by 2-foot by 2-foot recessed parabolic luminaires containing U-lamps. This type of coffer is also used in the history museum with an eggcrate baffle, which helps conceal adjustable spotlights and eliminate glare. The spotlights focus attention on artifacts in the museum's five segments devoted to stage coach transportation, express/freight service, banking, minerals and the history of southern California.

The lighting in all public areas and the board room are preset. Accent lighting is controlled by on/off switches to avoid distracting color shifts.

Track lights, recessed accent lights and downlights illuminate the reception area of the Wells Fargo History Museum.

WELCOME TO THE WELLS FARGO HISTORY MUSEUM

Artwork in the offices is not highlighted enough to demand full, constant, conscious attention, as art is in a museum. It is accented softly with recessed downlights and is viewed as an integral part of the environment.

In the reception area, the illumination from the pendant-mounted uplight fixtures is enough to render details and colors of the 22 × 27-foot oil-on-linen mural entitled "Stage" by John Farnsworth.

In the teller area of the branch bank, the custom-designed, indirect fixtures are suspended within ceiling coffers. Below, incandescent wallwashers illuminate the mural. Recessed fluorescent luminaires directly light the teller work area.

Lutheran Brotherhood Building

Lighting Designer: S. Leonard Auerbach,
S. Leonard Auerbach &
Associates, San Francisco,
CA

**Architect and
Interior Designer:** Skidmore, Owings & Merrill
Photographer: Balthazar Korab, Balthazar
Korab Ltd.
Client: Lutheran Brotherhood
Project Location: Minneapolis, MN
Award: 1984 IES Edwin F. Guth
Memorial Award of
Excellence

The variety of ceiling heights and shapes in the building was a challenge for the lighting designer. To illuminate the high-ceilinged lobby, 20 R-40 mercury vapor lamps with color correcting filters are column-mounted in sconces. Low-brightness fluorescent strips in a 12-inch diameter extrusion light the mezzanine-level library. This supplements the lobby illumination and accents the planters. In the lower-ceilinged elevator lobby, custom-designed low-brightness cylinder downlights add shine to the light-colored polished floor.

The magnificent vaulted ceiling and nonreflective interior materials made the corporate dining room difficult to light. The solution is a dual system. Continuous indirect coves smoothly illuminate the vault. Downlights recessed in the vault itself spotlight points of interest, such as the trees. The results are dramatic. Highly illuminated mesh against the dark-green, nonreflective background appears very crisp.

The performance/congregational facility is used for a variety of events, including religious services, music concerts and theatrical performances. All sources in this room are incandescent and quartz. They are controlled by a theatrical lighting system with multiplex controlled dimming. This allows a single control source for all functions and remote control locations for everyday use. The theatrical lighting is concealed in the perimeter of the ceiling. A series of incandescent bulbs echoes the rectangular shape of the room and adds sparkle and elegance to the understated interior design.

Large Japanese lanterns enclosing dimmed incandescent light sources are suspended from the ceiling of the executive dining rooms and add a touch of warmth.

Incandescent bulbs add sparkle to the neutral-toned performance/congregational facility.

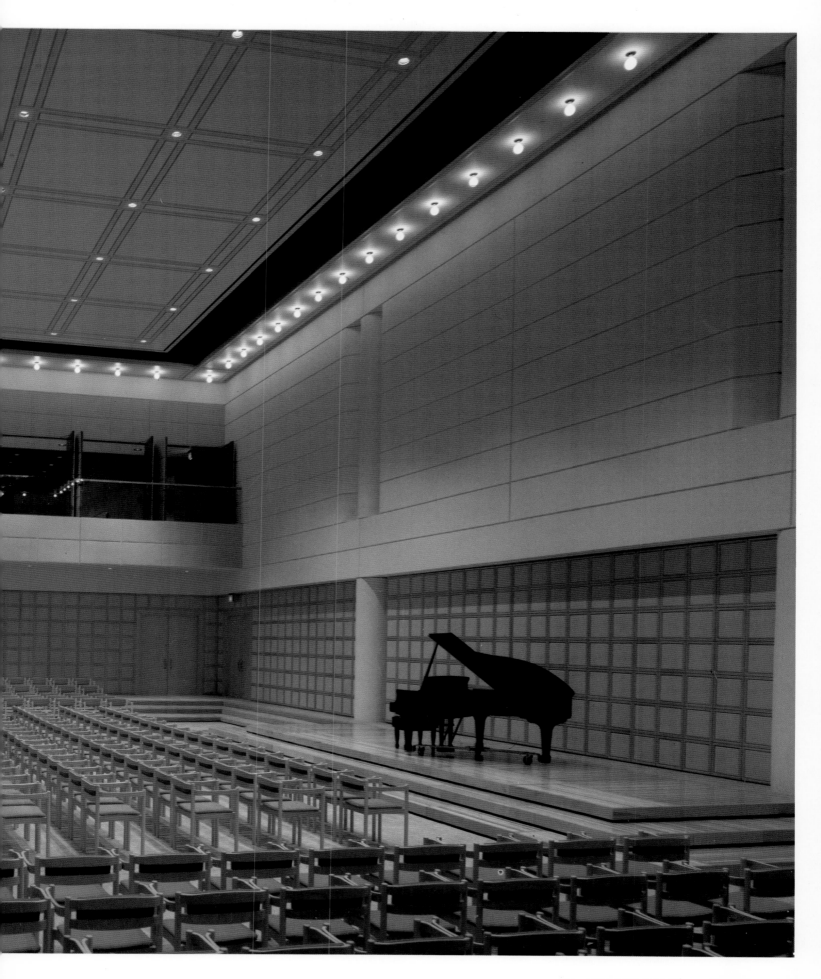

Indirect coves and recessed downlights are used in the vaulted corporate dining room.

Fidelity Bank

Lighting Designer: Lee Waldron, Grenald Associates, Ltd., Philadelphia, PA

Interior Designer: John Nelson, Nelson & Associates

Photographer: Tom Crane

Client: John McKelvie, Public Relations, Fidelcor, Inc.

Project Location: Philadelphia, PA

Award: 1985 IES Edwin F. Guth Award of Excellence

The renovation of Fidelity Bank, which took two years to complete, updated the style of the interiors and eliminated the feeling of confinement experienced by the growing staff. Many of the architectural details and becoming decorative fixtures were retained, refurbished and incorporated into the new design. For example, the white glass hemispherical fixtures that once graced the elevator lobbies have been cleaned, and the A lamps in them have been replaced with PL lamps to provide more light. They are now used in another area of the bank.

Flush-mounted ceiling downlights illuminate the lobby. Uplights mounted on the lobby walls reveal and highlight the beauty of preserved architectural ceiling details.

Offices and work areas, clustered around a central spine, are lighted by a fluorescent cove and troffer system. Perimeter walls do not need supplementary accenting because reflected light from the coves is sufficient. Work stations are equipped with parabolic, three-lamp fluorescent luminaires.

An atrium has been constructed in the center of the executive floor to encourage the impression of spaciousness. Since the atrium could not be skylighted due to spatial restrictions, cool-white deluxe fluorescent lamps are concealed in ceiling elements to produce an ambient glow.

In the board room, a custom-designed pendant-mounted luminaire is suspended from the 22-foot ceiling. The multi-purpose unit contains adjustable PAR-38 150-watt downlights on gimbal rings, which illuminate the conference table, and warm-white fluorescent lamps on the top of the fixture, which uplight the architectural details of the ceiling. The original wall sconces retain the flavor of the original interior design. Four different lighting schemes for the room are preset on computer.

Throughout the bank, PAR lamp downlights are used for accent and task lighting. The limited range of readily available light sources used throughout the installation aids maintenance of the system.

Curved archways complement the soft lines of the seating arrangement.

An atrium created in the executive office area creates a feeling of spaciousness.

The elevator bank before renovation.

The elevator bank after renovation. Incandescent downlights provide sufficient illumination for people and plantings.

The board rooms' custom-designed pendant luminaire contains both downlights and uplights.

The shape of the circular banquette is echoed in the overhead fluorescent cove.

Offices are clustered around a central spine.

Dae-Han Life Insurance Co., Ltd., Auditorium

Lighting Designer: Motoko Ishii, Motoko Ishii Lighting Design, Tokyo, Japan

Architects: Som & Associates, C.M. Park & Co.

Interior Designer: Sachio Shida, S. Shida Design Institute

Client: S.Y. Choi, Dae-Han Life Insurance Co., Ltd.

Project Location: Seoul, Korea

Award: 1986 IES Edwin F. Guth Memorial Special Citation

Elements of Korean culture are incorporated into the luminaires which cover the 25-foot high ceiling of the 85 × 111-foot auditorium in the company's 62-storey headquarters building. The sparkling chandeliers are modeled on the famous crown of the Shiragi Dynasty. Each chandelier is surrounded by curved louvers reminiscent of the traditional pleated dress of Korean women.

Diverse lighting effects, to suit the range of meetings, receptions and parties held in the space, are produced through combinations of two different features of the lighting system:

1. Illumination from the exposed and indirect incandescent colored reflector lamps is controlled and varied via a theatrical light board.

2. Motorized lifts raise or lower the chandeliers to achieve changes in the intensity of the colored light reflected onto the fanned louvers.

Here the pleated louvers are illuminated and the chandeliers have been dimmed.

A portion of the chandeliers have been lowered by motorized lifts.

Louvers left in darkness allow attention to be focused on the delicate design of the chandeliers.

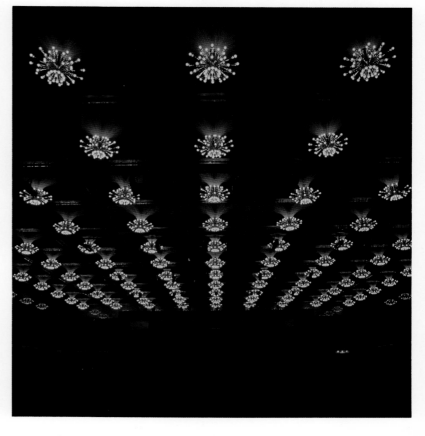

YKK50

Lighting Designer and Architect: Hidetoshi Ohno, APL Sogokeikaku Jimusho, Tokyo, Japan

Architects: Seiichi Endo and Shyuichi Kitamura, Endo Planning; Tadahiro Yoshida, Managing Director of YKK; Sadao Takasu, Section Chief of YKK Construction Department

Structural Eng., Lighting System Conference Hall: Toshihiko Kimura, Kimura Structural Engineers

Electrical Eng., Lighting System, Hall (advisor): Tuguo Endo, Sogo Setsubi Keikaku

Client: Tadao Yoshida, President, Yoshida Kogyo, KK

Project Location: Kurobe, Japan

Award: 1985 IALD Award of Excellence

The YKK50 Building is named in honor of the 50th anniversary of Yoshida Kogyo K K, a sliding fastener and sash manufacturing company. The building is the headquarters for the main factory in Kurobe, Japan. It is composed of two square wings joined by a central, glass-covered atrium. The large square contains an exhibition hall, offices and the International Conference Hall. The small square houses an exhibition hall, staff dining room and a banquet room. The atrium's bridge and stairway connect the two squares. At the back of the building is a memorial hall which displays Mr. Yoshida's great work.

An unusual approach was taken to design the facility. It is not the work of an individual architect or firm. It is the result of pooled efforts by a team of four architects, one structural engineer, one mechanical engineer and Mr. Yoshida, the eldest son of the founder, who was a member and leader of the group. The lighting designer joined this group in the final phase of the preliminary design stage.

The design process evolved by having each member bring his assigned work to an overall group meeting. The lighting designer was responsible for illumination of the guest meeting spaces, the banquet room, guest dining room, and reception area, as well as the general lighting system plan and the design of several fixtures.

The most difficult area to light was the International Conference Hall. The ceiling's diamond-shaped steel beams were exposed and allowed no space for recessing fixtures. Uplights were ruled out, because they would have cast unattractive "spider's web" shadows on the ceiling. The lighting fixture had to be accessible for maintenance in spite of the high dome and stepped floor. The acoustics of the conference hall also needed to be improved.

The solution is the creation of three large, suspended lighting fixtures, each capable of being raised or lowered by a motor for easy maintenance. Parallelogram lactescent acrylic panels, folded in a ribbed fashion to maintain rigidity, are incorporated into sturdy metal frames. Lamps are suspended behind the acrylic panels to produce soft, diffuse illumination. Although light is reflected to the ceiling by the panel, it does not create an unpleasant shadow because of the random directions of the rays that bounce off the ribs. The arbitrary shapes of the panels improved the acoustics of the room.

In the banquet room, the chandelier, suspended beneath a window, refracts slanting shafts of natural light and is composed of acrylic pipes and sticks. In the guest dining room, luminaires using Philippine sea shells on a steel frame adorn the elegant, residential-scale room.

The light poles designed for the atrium embody the industrial character of the company and bring the flavor of the outdoors into the space. They are used mainly as an element of the interior decoration, because primary nighttime illumination is provided by ceiling-mounted downlights. The stainless steel poles are topped by a fixture made of cast bronze and glass pipes which cups the light source.

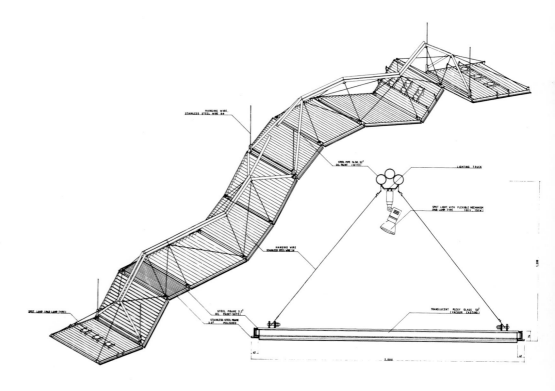

The three suspended lighting fixtures in the International Conference Hall are reminiscent of long strips of cloth trailing in the sky. There is a custom in Japan, called "Fukinagashi" that expresses poetical attachment to nature (sky and wind). It is represented by attaching a slender cloth to a tall bamboo pole during battle. It also symbolizes good wishes for a boy's growth into manhood.

The arches in the elevator lobby are inverted and repeated in the pole lights.

Downlights in the atrium provide main nighttime illumination. The pole lights are decorative and made of caste bronze, stainless steel and glass pipes.

A "rays of light" pattern is designed into the fixture for the banquet room. Japanese building regulations called for the fenestration above the luminaire.

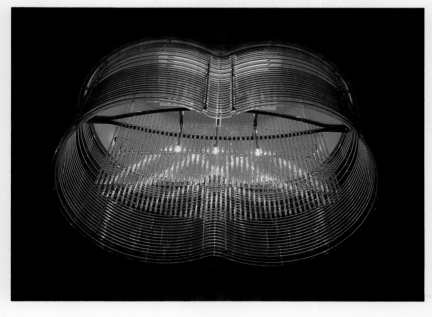

Calcasieu Aglow

Lighting Designer: Carroll D. Meyers, Lighting Associates, Inc., Houston, TX
Architect: Bob Philpot, Lloyd, Jones Philpot & Associates
Client: Calcasieu Marine National Bank
Project Location: Lake Charles, LA
Award: 1985 IES Edwin F. Guth Memorial Award of Excellence

The Calcasieu Marine National Bank is a high-rise office building associated with a three-storey bank building. An unusual approach was taken to illuminate the first floor banking area. Since penetrations into the 34-foot, fire-rated-height ceiling had to be minimized, a 10-foot-high teller island kiosk was designed with fixtures recessed, flush with the top. A 17,000-lumen metal halide, 3000-degree Kelvin clear lamp is positioned vertically in each housing, which measures 22⅛ inches front-to-back, 32⅜ inches long and 12⅝ inches deep. The ballast is also incorporated into the housing.

The fixtures are directed away from the view of staff and visitors using the second-storey walkway which looks down on the top of the kiosk. Baffling inside the luminaires also shields the lamps and prevents glare in the eyes of those looking down. Because the specular Alzak reflector is designed to project a beam pattern, a "donut" effect over the kiosk's center is eliminated. There is no additional, distracting brightness from the reflector, which appears gray in the daytime. An illumination level of 40 footcandles is achieved by these fixtures.

Standby lighting, to be used in the event of a power failure or for start-up, is accomplished by a 150-watt quartz lamp installed in each fixture that achieves a level of about 4 footcandles. The control relay is located in the box mounted on the ballast plate in the fixture.

Although ample illumination is provided by the indirect system on the tops of the tellers' workstations, supplementary lighting is used below their stations. To balance the "cloud of light" produced by the central kiosk system, a continuous fluorescent staggered strip is concealed in the foot railing and delineates the tellers' counter area. Behind the kiosk, bank officers receive uniform low-brightness illumination, which is supplemented at each of their workstations by furniture-mounted luminaires.

Trees and plantings, across the lobby from the kiosk, contribute a sense of warmth to the streamlined interior covered mainly with shiny, reflective materials. To keep the plantings flourishing, 250-watt, double-ended metal halide lamps in ellipsoidal framing projectors supply an excess of 500 footcandles without causing glare in the rest of the lobby. Each fixture is directed at a 45-degree angle to create the dramatic appearance of shafts of sunlight streaming through the leaves.

The fluorescent strip in the foot railing balances the indirect kiosk system above.

Each tree is framed with light by an ellipsoidal projector. Patterns cast on the floor add interest

A requirement of the architect was that the high-ceilinged bank be visible day and night from all points around Lake Charles. The "cloud of light" that glows the lobby satisfies this requirement.

Aetna Corporate Education Training Center

Lighting Designer: Jeffrey Milham, IALD, Design Decisions Inc., New York, NY

Architects: Jack Dollard, Aetna Life & Casualty; Jerry Lunt, Project Manager, DuBose Associates, Inc.

Mechanical/ Electrical Engineer: Paul Cramer, Legnos & Cramer Inc.

Photographer: Robert Benson

Client: Aetna Life & Casualty

Project Location: Hartford, CT

Award: 1984 IALD Honorable Mention

The architect envisioned a training center that would reflect Aetna's strong commitment to education. The lighting designer participated in the achievement of that vision. The six-storey building, which houses a dormitory and varied-sized classrooms, glows at night when illuminated and stands out as a landmark in the Hartford, Connecticut, landscape.

An indirect fluorescent system is used in the large, glass-enclosed lounges of the dormitory. Classrooms are lighted with tubular direct/indirect fluorescent units that provide functional lighting and attractively brighten the deeply coffered, exposed-concrete ceilings.

The classrooms are clustered around sky-lit atria. The atria are illuminated at night by industrial high-intensity discharge fixtures which also help to keep the plants thriving.

An open, airy feeling is created in the atrium by even illumination from high-intensity discharge luminaries.

The indirect fluorescent lighting helps to glow the building at night and to reveal its simple, grid-like pattern.

CHAPTER 2 HOTELS AND RESTAURANTS

One of the most important functions of lighting and interior design in both hotels and restaurants is their establishment of a distinctive image, or identity. While helping accomplish this, the lighting must also be flexible and easily maintained.

Hotels

The glamour of 1920s art deco has been recreated at the Omni Netherlands by refurbishing original decorative fixtures and relamping them with modern light sources for improved-quality output. The Wyndham Hotel blends both decorative fixtures—i.e., the 140-foot crystal chandelier in the atrium— and recessed fixtures—i.e., downlights in the lobby fitted with templates that project colored leaf patterns—to reflect an elegant, contemporary image. In the Fiesta Americana, cultural elements are drawn upon to instill in the public areas and restaurants the flavor of Mexico.

Whether it's a restoration, a contemporary-styled, or culturally-influenced design, a great deal of flexibility within the system can be achieved through the use of computers, controls and dimmers. Mood and atmosphere can be varied to correspond to time of day, and to suit special events and changing functions in public spaces, meeting rooms and restaurants. For example, at the Wyndham, the public areas are computer-programmed with eight different presets. Changes in the illumination levels take place gradually, over a 15-second period, so as not to disturb or distract guests. Hundreds of computer-operated fixtures can be directed to respond to the throbbing rhythms of disco and to display a vast range of kinetic effects in the Fiesta Americana. Controls and dimmers can extend lamp life, and reduce energy consumption and maintenance.

Maintenance is a key factor in the long-range success of any hotel design. It is every designer's hope that the lighting system will look as good, and operate as smoothly and effectively five years down the line as it does when it is first installed. Poor maintenance, the replacement of originally specified lamps with inadequate substitutes, and the failure to refocus or redirect fixtures when furnishings are rearranged can make the public areas of a hotel look shoddy and poorly planned.

Some design consultants instruct hotel staff on care and maintenance of the lighting system as part of their services. At the Wyndham, the designer intentionally limited the number of lamp types used to ease replacement. One of the design requirements for the Fiesta Americana was the use of low-maintenance, locally available lamps.

Restaurants

Flexibility, ease of maintenance and image creation apply to restaurants as well as hotels. At Calhoun's, beams from a simple, adjustable track system shine through nautical-style flags to foster the illusion that the tables are on a sunlit ship's deck.

Proper lighting in restaurants can both flatter the complexion of the diner, and make the food look more appetizing. Care must be taken to choose light sources which will render colors effectively.

One of the common problems in a poorly designed restaurant is that, in attempting to promote an intimate atmosphere, small pools of light are too sharply contrasted with shadow, causing the room to look uncomfortable and cavelike. Functional requirements must be compatibly blended with the "mood" effects desired. Diners should be able to read the menu without straining; to see something of the surrounding environment in order to feel relaxed, secure and comfortable; and to locate quickly pathways to and from entryways, salad bars, telephones and restrooms.

Two restaurants featured in this chapter create intimate atmospheres even though the sizes of the rooms are very different. In Sushi-Zen, three lighting systems illuminate tables, pathways and surroundings, and also manage to make the long, narrow space seem wider than it really is. In the Palm Court of the Omni Netherlands Hotel, eye-level elements are used to establish a sense of intimacy in the large, high-ceilinged space that was once used as a lobby.

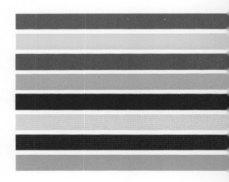

Fiesta Americana Hotel, Tijuana

Lighting Designers: Lawrence Silverman, Chris Harms, principals; C. Landhart, D. Salome, H. Osuma, assoc. des.; Transtek Int'l. Ltd., Philadelphia, New York, El Paso

Photographers: L. Silverman, L. Lindauer

Client: Fiesta Americana Hotel, Tijuana

Project Location: Tijuana, Mexico

Award: 1986 IES Edwin F. Guth Memorial Award of Excellence

The sleek, glass exterior of the five-star, luxury Fiesta Americana Hotel, Tijuana, is complemented by an equally modern, high-style interior. The latest, state-of-the-art lighting equipment is used in the hotel's discotheque, which is designed to appeal both to visiting young, international jet-setters and to more conservative local clientele.

In addition to disco dancing, the room is used for movie viewing, fashion shows, music and sports video viewing, live entertainment, cocktail receptions, parties and special events. The lighting system had to be flexible, varied and exciting enough to serve all those purposes in a sophisticated, tasteful style.

Restrictions and client requirements confronting the lighting team included:

1. Use of only low-maintenance, locally available lamps.

2. Minimal consumption of electricity.

3. Limited space available for lighting equipment, due to several large plumbing and air-conditioning ducts running across the ceiling and rear wall of the dance floor.

4. A budget made in accordance with a required 18-month payback.

One of the highlights of the space, and key to the success of the lighting system, is a tiered ceiling soffit which echoes the shape of the semi-circular dance floor below it. Equipment is both revealed for effect and concealed behind the tiered ceiling.

Four circuits of colored neon, recessed above each tier, wash the vertical surfaces of the soffit. The kinetic visual display of neon can be seen by dancers below. The modulus of four circuits maximizes the use of the off-the-shelf controls—separate hot and neutral runs increase switching flexibility. Ductwork is hidden behind the tiers.

Shafts of light, from low-voltage pinbeams mounted with pipeclamps above the tiers, shine through holes fitted with detachable downlight trims. Moving effects, ellipsoidal spots and downlights are contained in a semi-circular steel support that slants inward along the outside of the dance floor ceiling. This support grid is masked by an enclosing 3-foot semi-circular dropped soffit, into which also are recessed theatrical scoops in four colors used for broad color washes over the dance floor. The outer-perimeter soffit houses both inward-directed bass and midrange speakers as well as other sound and lighting effects used over the floor.

Another highlight of the space is the back wall of the dance floor, which is covered with glass block to conceal the special lighting effects equipment and the ductwork behind it. In the center of the wall is a semi-circular column. Four angled vertical panels on each side of the column create a feeling of architectural motion.

Floor-to-ceiling color washes, due to the limited space behind the glass block, are produced by backbounce of light. Striking, vibrant colors are combined for a myriad of effects. For example, saturated red and blue neon patterns contrast with soft, pastel, back wall washes. One particularly stunning effect is achieved at low cost—a deep icy blue-purple glow over the entire rear wall made by F40-BLB blacklights placed behind the angled panels and central column.

Additional kinetic effects are provided by strobe lights, oscillators and rotating beacons. The rippling patterns caused by the distorting and diffusing of colored light through the glass block make it difficult for dancers to identify the light source and adds to the magic and mystery of the space.

An unexpected special effect comes from the bottom row of the glass block wall. Rectangular car headlights, in standard automotive retaining hardware, are positioned there. When off, they look like glass bricks. When switched on, the flat horizontal beams blast through fog at floor level and onto dancers' feet. Louvered vents for the fog machine outlets are interspersed around the floor.

Tubelight is routed in a pattern in the dance floor, outlines the vertical edges of the glass block wall panels, runs along the perimeter edges of the ceiling tiers, and is used as understep security lighting throughout the room and at the main entrance.

All the lighting is connected to programmable controls. Standard electronic components are used as modular building-blocks configured by the designers into an overall system. A pushbutton preset dimming controller engineered and supplied by the lighting designer provides varied architectural lighting setups for the room.

The light sources chosen (neon, low-voltage and tubelight) are low maintenance and low energy consuming. Combined with the controls and dimmer, lamplife is extended, energy consumption and required maintenance are reduced, and flexibility is increased. The room is in use 70 to 80 hours a week. The Fiesta Americana Hotel Tijuana was officially inaugurated by Miguel de la Madrid, President of Mexico, on February 15, 1986.

The atrium's "indoor sidewalk cafe" reflects the French influence in Mexican culture, which dates back to the 1860s, when the country was ruled by a French emperor.

The atrium chandelier contains more than
20,000 bud lights. At its longest point, it is
about 50 feet.

The traditionally styled Mexican restaurant is enhanced by vaulted ceilings. Some coves are lit with neon. Folk art objects displayed in the wall niches are highlighted with MR-16 lamps.

The hotel cafe has an unusual alternating vaulted ceiling. The walls are uplighted by decorative wall sconces. In the center of the room, a 6-foot high uplight luminaire is equipped with high-wattage quartz lamps to provide soft coloring.

The steps and parts of the walls in the gourmet restaurant are composed of unique rear-illuminated onyx. A crystal chandelier is suspended from a vaulted cove in the center of the room.

A 60-foot wall washed mural depicting a turn-of-the-century scene on the Place de la Concorde in Paris in photo-realistic style adorns one wall of the gourmet restaurant. In all the restaurants and meeting rooms, lighting is computer-controlled with preset dimmers.

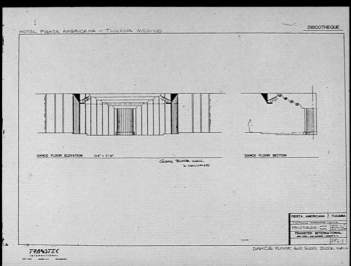

Side and full view plans of the disco dance floor.

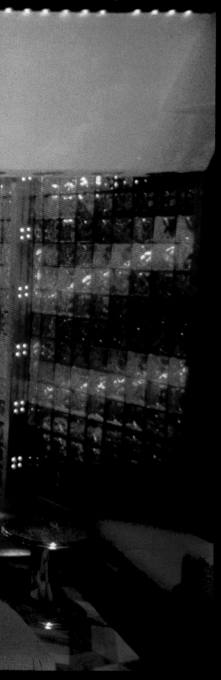

The tiered soffits contain both revealed and concealed lighting equipment. They echo the semi-circular shape of the dance floor.

The room is not only used as a disco, but for fashion shows, movie viewing, live entertainment, cocktail receptions, parties and special events. The lighting system had to be flexible enough to accommodate all of these events.

Four circuits of neon recessed above each tier wash the vertical surfaces of the soffits. Changing patterns and colors are achieved on the glass block wall through backlighting and backbounce.

The bottom row of the glass block wall contains rectangular car headlights, the beams from which blast through fog at floor level.

Omni-Netherlands Hotel

Lighting Designer: John Aspromonte, principal in charge, Wheel Gersztoff Friedman Associates, Inc., New York, NY

Architect: Richard Rauh, Rabun, Hatch, Portman, McWhorter, Hatch & Rauh Inc., Atlanta, GA

Interior Designers: Rita St. Clair, Val Peratt Restoration of Decorative Fitting by Cincinnati Plating Co.

Photographer: Norman McGrath

Client: Ellison Emery Development Corp.

Project Location: Cincinnati, OH

Award: 1986 IES Edwin F. Guth Memorial Award of Excellence

The restoration of the Omni-Netherlands Hotel (formerly the Netherlands Plaza) brought to life again the art deco detailing of the original interiors by Rita St. Clair. The new lighting had to complement the 1920's "look" while incorporating modern concepts and techniques.

Originally, the lobby lounge was lighted by wall sconces and by uplights built into a huge center table. The even illumination it produced was standard 50 or so years ago, but would not appear glamorous to today's hotel guest.

To appeal to current tastes and to suit the changed function of the room (it now houses the Palm Court Restaurant), an interplay of light and shadow was created that achieves a sense of drama and intimacy in the 30-foot high ceilinged space.

On the ceiling, only the decorative panels are highlighted with 120 PAR-64, 6-volt narrow spot lamps (one per panel), which are shielded by a slightly diffuse lens to soften the beam pattern. The portions of the ceiling in between the panels are subdued in shadow. The fixtures are tucked against balcony rails on the mezzanine level, and since they are directed upward, go unnoticed by first-floor visitors.

Eye-level elements are used to foster the sense of intimacy. Backlighting of the oversized, fan-shaped banquettes, which line the walls in most areas of the room, highlights the rich wood paneling, and brings out the details of the glistening metal sconces. Wiring had to be replaced and all metal panels polished and refinished in all the large decorative wall sconces. Most of the A lamps used in the sconces had been partially blocked by the metal panels. By moving the sockets forward and changing from A lamps to R-20 lamps, the effect of the chandeliers was doubled.

A huge floral display in the core of two assemblies of banquettes is uplighted by a ring of R-20 lamps recessed below a louver grill underneath the centerpiece. A luminous bar canopy attracts attention to the center of the Palm Court.

Shown is the lobby before restoration. The designers of the 1920's did not concern themselves with light and shadow as designers do today. The illumination was provided by brightly lighted wall sconces.

The original art deco detailing was brought back. The interiors are true to the spirit of the original hotel.

The 120 PAR-64 lamps point upward to illuminate the ceiling and do not cause distracting glare. Wall sconces contain R-20 lamps. The luminous bar canopy can be seen in the center of the Palm Court.

Illumination of the ceiling area reveals the rich materials and decorative art and creates a bright, open atmosphere.

Recessed downlights reveal and enhance the ornate details of the interior.

Sushi-Zen Restaurant

Lighting Designer and Architect: David Rockwell and Jay Haverson, Haverson/Rockwell Architects, PC, New York, NY

Silk Mural Created By: Donna Granata

Photographer: Mark Ross, Mark Ross Photography

Client: Carl and Kim Shiraishi and Toshio Suzuki

Project Location: New York, NY

Award: 1986 IES Edwin F. Guth Memorial Award of Distinction

The challenge for the designer was to create the illusion that the long, narrow room (18 feet, 6 inches by 56 feet) was open and spacious, yet tranquil and intimate. To achieve these purposes, three lighting systems were designed:

1. Gentle pools of light in the floor establish the pathway and public zone and make the space seem wider than it is. These are created from glass block uplit with 4-foot fluorescent lamps placed every one-and-a-half feet in between the floor joists. A neutral density filter is used to achieve the appropriate lighting level, as this system, unlike the other two, is not dimmable. Little maintenance is required.

2. At the dining tables and the sushi bar, a mixture of narrow and very narrow 12-volt, 50-watt spotlights project focal points for the diners. The small circles of light surrounded by shadow contribute to the feeling of intimacy. The dimmable low-voltage incandescent accent lights also render the colors of the food very well.

3. The three-dimensional silk mural by Donna Granata is highlighted with dimmable continuous neon color washes which are semi-concealed, so that the emphasis remains on the mural.

Changes from lighter to darker areas are gradual, not jarring. The blacked-out ceiling combines with the focal points of light on the tables to create a sense of intimacy.

The crisp, modern style of the interior is revealed first
in the entryway. "Sushi Zen" attracts attention, and the
color adds life without overwhelming.

The angularity of the sushi bar, raised two steps from the main dining floor, adds interest to the space. Subtle blues, pinks and beiges offer a feeling of tranquility.

Wyndham Hotel

Lighting Designer: Craig A. Roeder, Craig A. Roeder Associates, Inc., Dallas and Houston, TX
Architect: Dahl, Braden & Chapman, Inc.
Interior Designer: TC Design and Construction Co.
Photographer: Robert Ames Cook
Client: Wyndham Hotel
Project Location: Dallas, TX
Award: 1983 IALD Honorable Mention

The 542-room hotel provides guests with a spectacular surprise upon entry. Suspended by aircraft cable from the top of the four-storey atrium to the basement level, where executive offices are located, is a 140-foot long chandelier. It is composed of 7,500 Venetian triadri crystals and 250 40-watt tubular incandescent lamps (9,000 watts total). Both of these hang from a bronze aluminum frame. Its coil shape mimics the oval, winding staircase that surrounds it. The appearance of the sparkling, delicate crystals and the free-wheeling winding pattern belie the chandelier's 7,000-pound weight. It is cleaned from the stairway, and the lamps, which have a three-year life, are refitted all at once.

In addition to the chandelier, the lighting in the public areas on the first three floors was specially designed. In the registration lobby, 300-watt quartz recessed downlights are fitted with glass templates to project pink and lavender leaf patterns on the travertine floors. The same patterns are used on the bar top of the second floor lounge.

Throughout the hotel, wall-washers highlight artwork and fabric-covered walls. Low-voltage units are used wherever possible to conserve energy. Though 30 different fixtures are installed, the number of lamps is limited to approximately 12, to ease the task of maintaining the elegant, well-planned atmosphere.

Eight different lighting programs for public areas—breakfast, lunch, dinner, special events, parties, cleanup, and general day and evening levels—are preset on computer. In the second floor lounge, for example, rose-colored daytime lighting is scheduled to change to blue-toned illumination at night. Individual areas can depart from the preset via dimmer switches and a manual override. So as not to distract or disturb guests, each lighting level "changeover" takes place gradually and is almost unnoticed over a 15-second period.

Leaf patterns are projected onto the travertine floor in the lobby. Glass templates are fitted on 300-watt quartz recessed downlights.

The 140-foot long atrium chandelier contains 7,500
Venetian triadri crystals and 250 tubular incandescent
lamps.

Calhoun Ltd.

Lighting Designer: Dennis R. Jones, Dennis R. Jones Associates, Richardson, TX
Interior Designers: Harold Young, AIA, ASID, and Bob Sowell, ASID, Architectural Designers, Inc.
Photographer: Bob Sowell, ASID
Client: Calhoun Beach Club Inc.
Project Location: Minneapolis, MN
Award: 1986 Halo/SPI National Lighting Competition First Place Winner

Calhoun's restaurant overlooks Calhoun Lake, a summer sailing center in Minneapolis. A nautical theme is carried through the 4,832-square-foot space using nautical flags, wood deck flooring and deck furniture.

Lighting is the key element in the creation of the sunny ship-deck atmosphere that lasts all year round here, even in the bitter cold and cloudy winters. Track lights installed on 4-circuit tracks are positioned to shine through and between the silk flags like the sun's rays. The flags also serve to keep the track system concealed and unobtrusive. White furnishings and light-colored walls reflect illumination and amplify the brightness.

Light from track units filters down through silk nautical flags and mimics the sun's rays.

CHAPTER 3   MERCHANDISE

The lighting system in a merchandise area or store must fulfill several basic requirements. It must:

1. Highlight the merchandise to its best advantage. This includes avoiding conditions such as glare, extreme shadow or poor color rendering that would interfere with the customer's ability to evaluate realistically items on display.

2. Provide a sufficient level and quality of illumination in areas where customers are permitted to handle and examine items closely. One area of primary importance in a clothing store that is often overlooked is the fitting or dressing room. One of the most common occurrences is inadequate illumination or use of light sources which render clothing colors very differently than the sources in the environment in which the items will be worn. Designers can help make owners aware of the need for better lighting in fitting rooms, where the customer frequently makes the final decision on whether or not to buy.

3. Be flexible enough to accommodate changing displays, and easy enough for store employees to adjust and/or maintain.

These requirements can be fulfilled in a variety of ways, several of which are featured in this chapter. Track lighting systems are popular because of the flexibility they offer and the attention-getting highlighting effect they achieve by focusing pools of light directly on the merchandise.

At Franco Ferrini Shoes, the intense tungsten-halogen track units add vividness to the appearance of the shoes and accessories and make supplementary ambient light unnecessary.

Uniform lighting systems can also present merchandise effectively. The simple, elegant design of Santini e Dominici's interior is complemented by a luminous ceiling punctuated with sparkling Italian low-voltage halogen lamps.

Lighting fixtures can either be concealed or purposely left visible to complement the interior design or architecture. At the Joslin, Loyd Paxton and Haddonstone showrooms, fixtures are painted black and placed as unobtrusively as possible so that attention may be directed solely to the merchandise.

At the Donna Karan Showroom and the Esprit Store, the lighting fixtures, visible to the clientele, enhance the overall styles of the interiors.

Showrooms can differ from other merchandise areas because they must appeal to the sophisticated, professional designers or buyers who are often their clientele. Two approaches to both showroom and general merchandise display are presented here.

The first approach is to incorporate the objects to be sold into a specially-created, artificial or theme setting. For example, at the Joslin Showroom, the lighting and

architectural elements are reminiscent of ancient ruins beneath a star-studded night sky. This dramatic, intriguing backdrop is juxtaposed with the office furnishings displayed. In the E.F. Hauserman Showroom, the product is incorporated into a one-of-a-kind light art show, which plays upon the viewer's perception of form and perspective.

A second approach is to display the products in a setting similar to the one in which they will be used

after purchase. At the Loyd Paxton Galleries, incandescent illumination similar to that found in the homes of the gallery's clientele highlights furniture and small art objects that are arranged realistically in personal, roomlike displays. At the Haddonstone Show Gardens, the stonework, columns, urns and fountains are displayed in the type of beautiful outdoor garden in which they will ultimately be placed.

Franco Ferrini Shoes

Lighting Designer: Jan Lennox Moyer, Luminae, Inc., San Francisco, CA
Architect: John Gall, Foothill Design Group
Interior Designer: Karen Kitowski
Photographer: James Benya, Luminae, Inc.
Developer: Robert Powell, The Robert Powell Company
Client: Shaw Deghan, Franco Ferrini
Project Location: Sacramento, CA
Award: 1985 GE Edison Award

Since there was no plenum space available for lighting equipment, the designer exposed the lighting system and incorporated it into the modern, high-style "look" of the shop's interior design. The ceiling-mounted track system uses 75-watt MR-16 lamps. Its adjustability accommodates the ever-changing displays of shoes, handbags and other accessories. The sparkle and compactness of the intense tungsten-halogen lamps are in keeping with the delicate, streamlined design of the interior. The source's rich color rendition adds vividness and richness to the appearance of the merchandise. Ambient light is unnecessary, and the lack of it keeps attention dramatically focused on the merchandise.

The same lamps with tinted gels added create visual impact, reveal texture and heighten three-dimensionality in the window display. Shelf lighting is accomplished by 12-volt incandescent strip lights with 5-W lamps and remote 12-volt transformers.

This high-quality shoe store had to be designed and installed in eight weeks on a limited budget. It met strict California energy code requirements of 1.5 watts per square foot.

The modern, clean look of the lamps matches the contemporary design of the shop.

The display shelves on rollers occasionally are moved and repositioned.

The ceiling lacks any space for recessing fixtures. The small shop is only 19 by 28 feet.

Pools of light keep attention directed to the shoes, while pathways are in shadow.

Esprit Store

Lighting Designer: Alfred Scholze, Alfred Scholze Associates, Santa Monica, CA
Interior Designer: Joseph D'Urso, Joseph D'Urso Co.
Photographer: Alfred Scholze
Clients: Doug and Susie Tompkins, Esprit De Corp.
Project Location: Los Angeles, CA
Award: 1986 IALD Award of Excellence

The 43,000-square-foot Esprit Store is housed in a building that was originally a bowling alley built by Art Linkletter in the 1930's. The store is divided into five different areas—children's clothes, sportswear, shoes, accessories and the main selling area—each with its own distinctive character and style. The lighting designers were requested to provide a different style for each department that would complement the architectural elements as well.

The lighting systems installed use a wide variety of lamps and fixtures. For example, in the children's area 200-watt PAR-46 lamps are contained in modified fixtures clamped to a ceiling-mounted pipe grid system and individually plugged into ceiling-mounted outlets. In the main selling area, 300-watt PAR-46 luminaires are used. Fluorescent fixtures illuminate the stocking area and 250-watt metal halide units are installed in the office.

Though much of the lighting equipment is visible to the customer, the pipes, housings and some architectural elements are painted black to form a neutral background for the brightly colored and patterned clothes and accessories.

The strong lines and patterns of the lighting elements overhead, and in some areas the sheer mass of them, create an excitement appealing to the young and spirited clientele. The jury granting the award for the store noted the attention paid to the fixtures, the successfully-created impression of "controlled chaos" in the ceiling areas, and the common themes employed in the architecture and the lighting. The illumination system is flexible and operates within California's strict Title 24 energy usage limitations.

Light sources were chosen that would render the colors of the youth-oriented merchandise brightly and vividly.

In a section of the main selling area, specially-designed black shopping carts are made available for customers to wheel about and collect items for purchase. The check-out counters are designed to look like those at a supermarket.

In the shoe area, a large, sculptured form serves as a display on which shoes rest.

Some architectural elements and fixtures are painted black to form a neutral backdrop for the varied-colored merchandise.

The store is divided into five areas: children's clothes, sportswear, shoes, accessories and the main selling area.

Though hundreds of fixtures are used — 300 in the sports area alone — they are not all up to 100 percent all the time. Ninety percent of the fixtures can be dimmed and controlled by computer.

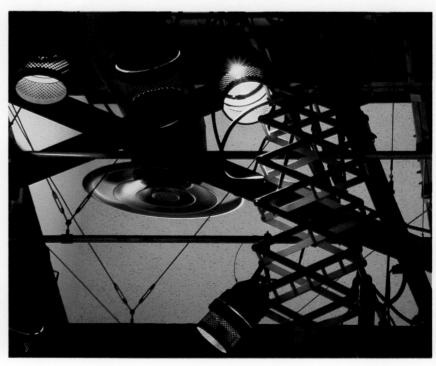

The wall-mounted displays in the sports area reinforce the concept of the store as a "clothes supermarket" in which entire ensembles can be coordinated and purchased. ➤

Via the lighting, attention is drawn to the merchandise and displays. Pathways are left in gentle shadow.

A different style of lighting was designed for each of the five areas of the store.

The giant posters provide examples of ensemble combinations and add vertical brightness, color and interest to the space.

The novel, controlled-chaos effect of the maze of fixtures and architectural elements is designed to appeal to the spirited clientele.

Flexibility is built into the system to accommodate frequently-changing merchandise. A staff person at Esprit has been trained to adjust fixtures and operate the computer.

Santini e Dominici

Lighting and Interior Designer: Les Beilinson, Beilinson Architect, P.A., Miami, FL
Photographer: Seth Benson
Client: Mrs. Susan Tauber, Santini e Dominici
Project Location: Miami, FL
Award: 1985 IES Edwin F. Guth Memorial Award of Excellence

Santini e Dominici is located in the Bal Harbour Shops mall which caters to upscale customers. The shoe company's elegant, 600-square-foot interior incorporates a multi-colored striped logo. Due to the brightness and vividness of logo colors, repeated in the array of merchandise, the lighting system had to provide good color rendition.

The planned lighting system uses two light sources. An even, diffuse illumination is produced by a luminous ceiling made up of ribbed glass panels sandblasted to conceal deluxe warm white fluorescent tubes. The panels are suspended by a custom-fabricated aluminum frame, painted black for contrast.

A second lighting element, an Italian low-voltage halogen lamp supplied by the owner, had to be incorporated into the plan. The lamps have been modified by the designer with glass insulators to meet U.L. requirements. These halogen units are suspended in two rows of glass opaline panels. The dual-source system renders color well and enhances the refined, quality image of the shop.

To eliminate shadows completely and to promote uniform illumination, reflective surfaces—a white marble floor and white opaline glass walls—are used throughout the space. The totally glowing space suits both fixed and moveable displays. Joints in the marble, opaline glass and ceiling are articulated to relate to each other and to unify the design of the interior.

The interior provides a neutral backdrop for the brightly-colored logo and merchandise.

Even, shadowless illumination is achieved with a fluorescent luminous ceiling and low-voltage halogen lamps.

Donna Karan Showroom

Lighting Designer: Robert Stortz, FTL Associates, New York, NY

Architect: Nicholas Goldsmith, FTL Associates

Photographer: Elliott Kaufman, Elliott Kaufman Photography

Client: Donna Karan, Donna Karan Corp.

Project Location: New York, NY

Award: 1985 IALD Honorable Mention

The garment district showroom is used for small fashion shows as well as customer sales. It is designed with a collage-like, chaotic background of dark, angled fabric and metal grids to counterbalance the simple lines of Donna Karan's fashions.

The lighting designer, an experimenter in the use of fabric structures, created a pair of peaked and curved custom-fabricated wings from flame-treated nylon material. The structures, suspended from the ceiling beneath light sources, yield bright, but diffuse, ambient illumination. The light's good color balance and softened, even tones are appreciated by photographers who take pictures during the fashion shows.

The small center area, used for fashion shows, is evenly illuminated by fabric "wings" and is suitable for taking photographs.

Angular background elements of varied textures contrast with the smooth textures and simple lines of the clothing.

E.F. Hauserman Showroom

Interior Designers: Lella and Massimo Vignelli, principals-in-charge; David Law and Michele Kolb, design team, Vignelli Associates, New York, NY

Light Artist: Dan Flavin; Robert Skolnik, supervisor of installation

Engineers: (for Hauserman) Charles Saylor, vice president; William Peterson, facilities designer; Ray Baggs, construction supervisor

General Contractor: G.J. Krause Co.

Client: E.F. Hauserman Co.

Photographer: Toshi Yoshimi

Project Location: Los Angeles, CA

Award: 1983 IES Edwin F. Guth Memorial Award of Distinction

The Hauserman Showroom, located in the Pacific Design Center in Los Angeles, was designed:

1) to display to its best advantage the company's main product—office partitions

2) to embody and express the forward-thinking image of the company and its commitment to art and experimentation.

The interior designer decided to highlight the partitions, which usually are viewed only as background elements, by making them part of a "light show." Instead of containing the ordinary office-situation vignettes, common in most showrooms, the Hauserman space was divided into three corridors, angled at 45 degrees and composed of light-colored panels, matched carefully with a smooth, bleached-oak floor. Two corridors on either side are barred at the mid-point, so they can be viewed from either end, but not walked through. The central corridor is left open.

Light artist, Dan Flavin, created the artistic treatment of the panels using color-filtered fluorescent tubes. The first corridor is bisected by a horizontal light barrier that is yellow on one side and pink on the other. The middle corridor is filled with blue-colored tubes placed in an angular, spiraling pattern. The third corridor contains obliquely-placed green tubes which yield to yellow. A mirrored wall at the rear of the corridors reflects borrowed light, and repeats the illusory colored light and angles.

An introductory corridor, on a perimeter wall apart from the "light show," is used to display the company's range of panel materials and colors. There is a small conference room/office and a presentation room, both with neutral-toned, simple furnishings.

The focus in the minimally-furnished reception area is on the giant-sized words "the Walls" rendered in white on a light-colored panel, which remind the visitor that the colorful art spectacle seen within is really a unique, distinctive and novel showcase for the company's primary product. Here is a successful blending of art and merchandise display.

The custom desk in the reception area is made with the same bleached oak used for the flooring.

In the entryway, giant-sized letters announce the true focus of the showroom — the "Walls."

Three corridors in the central portion of the showroom are angled at 45 degrees.

View looking back toward the entryway. The partitions purposely are neutral-colored to form an appropriate backdrop for the multi-colored light show.

The third corridor is bisected by a horizontal light barrier, yellow on one side and pink on the other.

The central corridor contains a spiral of blue-filtered fluorescent tubes.

Dan Flavin's art increases the awareness of, and changes the perception of, color and space. The unique approach to designing the showroom was taken to complement the company's forward-thinking concern with art and experimentation.

Vertical fluorescent tubes set obliquely, green yielding to yellow.

The projection room is furnished in nondistracting
neutral tones.

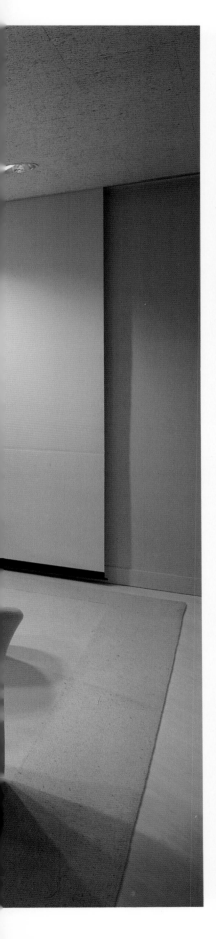

At the rear of the showroom, a mirrored wall reflects light and form.

Roger Joslin and Company Showroom

Lighting and Interior Designer, Architect: Mark Eubank, AIA, RTG/Partners, Inc., Austin, TX

Photographer: R. Greg Hursley, R. Greg Hursley, Inc.

Client: Roger Joslin, Roger Joslin & Company

Project Location: Austin, TX

Award: 1986 Halo/SPI National Lighting Competition First Place Winner

Track lighting looks like stars in a night sky. The levels of grout markings are visible on the columns.

The client wanted a showroom that would help promote and sell his line of custom-made office furnishings, cabinetry and millwork. This had to be achieved on a very moderate budget in a relatively small space.

The design solution is geared around freestanding architectural elements, resembling the columns and archways of ancient ruins. These are placed in a diagonal grid to break up and draw the customer interestingly through the long, narrow space. The repetition of the architectural forms maintains visual continuity and creates personal, room-like settings.

Narrow and medium beam low-voltage, high-intensity fixtures are focused on the carefully-placed furniture. The flexible track system offers maximum control at minimum cost.

The spill light from these units softly highlights portions of the freestanding elements, leaving the remainder in shadow. The mood of mystery, fostered by the play of light and shadow, is reinforced by the black ceiling and the concrete floor which is painted black and scored with a grid pattern. The fixtures sparkle as if in a night sky. The freestanding forms loom in the background, and the ceiling and floor tend to disappear, allowing full attention to be drawn to the furniture.

An effort was made to use materials in an effective, but not necessarily orthodox fashion. The texture of stone is simulated on the architectural elements by using a durable liquid vinyl paint. Stripes are painted on the columns to represent grout lines. Two lines on columns are placed intentionally at 30 inches (desk and window sill height) and 102 inches (the height of the standard office ceiling). This enables customers to relate to the scale and better visualize the furnishings in their offices. At the rear of the showroom, mirrors and reflective vertical blinds provide depth and dimension, conceal work areas and visually help to enlarge the space.

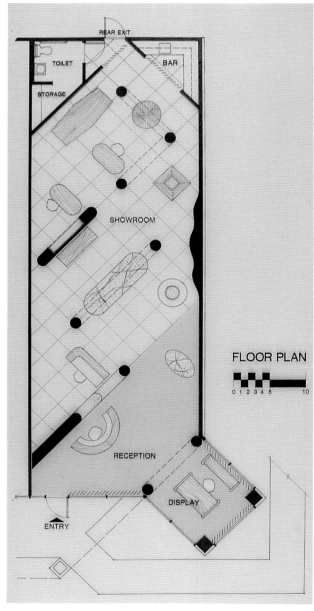

FLOOR PLAN

0 1 2 3 4 5   10

Floor plan.

Lighting focuses on the furniture. The spill light leaves
the architectural forms half in shadow, creating a
mood of mystery.

The architectural elements divide the 1,592-square-foot
space into more personal "rooms".

Loyd-Paxton Galleries and Residence

Lighting Designer: Craig A. Roeder, Craig A. Roeder Associates, Inc., Dallas and Houston, TX
Architect: Hendricks and Wall
Interior Designer: Charles Paxton Gremillion
Photographer: Robert Ames Cook
Clients: Loyd Ray Taylor and Charles Paxton Gremillion
Project Location: Dallas, TX
Award: 1986 Edwin F. Guth Memorial Award of Excellence (for exterior and gallery lighting)

A beautiful blending of old and new aptly describes the Loyd Paxton Galleries. Precious antiques—English, French and Continental furnishings and art objects—are revealed by the most modern and technologically up-to-date illumination and control systems available.

Pole lighting for the exterior was ruled out because it is forbidden by city ordinance, and the building is under 10 feet from the property line. The designer chose to create a strong visual identification for the building by uplighting the columns with custom-designed burial units installed flush with the ground. To avoid build-up of debris or damage to the fixture, the designer worked with the manufacturer to develop an internal louver recessed three inches below the ground in an unobtrusive black matte finish. The inside louver prevents glare from hitting the eyes of passersby and directs light onto the neutral-colored facade. An atmosphere of festiveness and excitement is created for special occasions by placing colored glass filters on top of the louvers—for example, red and green for Christmas, or yellow and red for a Mexican fiesta. Lamps used in the first floor burial units are 250-watt quartz PAR-38 flood lamps. They provide superior beam spread and intensity. On the second floor residential terrace, 150-watt quartz PAR-38 lamps produce softer illumination.

The luminaires are on a time clock which is controlled by a dimming computer and activated by a photocell.

The exterior and the interior are painted the same shade of taupe so customers experience a smooth visual continuity as they move inside the building and from gallery to gallery. The neutral color also allows full attention to be focused on the furniture and art objects.

The limited ceiling space available for recessing fixtures, and the need to refocus fixtures as merchandise is sold and displays are changed, led the designer to install a flexible, high-grade track system in the galleries. Two tracks run parallel to each of the four walls

in every gallery. The two-circuit tracks, mounted 2 feet from the walls, are equipped with 12-volt, 50-watt very narrow pin spots with self-contained transformers (120-volt lamps can also be used). The two-circuit tracks 4 feet from the walls use 150-watt PAR-38 spot and flood lamps. Deep hoods and internal louvers on all the fixtures shield lamps from view at all angles except from directly ahead. The black matte ceiling and housings allow the track system to go virtually unnoticed by clientele. The quality of the light produced is comparable to the illumination provided in the fine homes in which the merchandise will be displayed.

Also on the first floor is an operations area, which includes offices, kitchen, shipping and receiving. These spaces are illuminated with 2 foot by 2 foot parabolic fluorescent luminaires.

Energy-saving, low-voltage fixtures are used in coves and display cabinets. For example, coves are equipped with two rows of 24-volt strip lights that contain incandescent "peanut" lamps.

Though the interior of the building contains over 5,500 lamps, only two or three a week require changing. The gallery staff notes fixtures requiring maintenance on a worksheet. Someone from the lighting consultant's office visits the installation twice each month to adjust and refocus equipment.

Residential areas, which include the entire second floor, and a conference/dining room and library on the first floor, are illuminated with recessed low-voltage fixtures fitted with a variety of PAR-36 and very narrow spot lamps. The gallery owners carefully placed furniture and objects before lighting was installed so light would be applied only where it is needed.

The interior lighting systems are controlled by a sophisticated computer system.

Each circuit in the house, gallery and exterior can be dimmed simultaneously from any control station. Each room can be dimmed independently as well from its own control panel.

The clients worked closely with the designer to set several appropriate light levels. The most often used settings are 80 percent full and an energy-saving level of about 70 percent.

Lighting levels are purposely coordinated from one gallery to another so no distracting transitions occur.

Colored glass filters can be fitted onto the recessed exterior fixtures for special occasions.

Burial units on the second floor residential terrace are equipped with 150-watt quartz PAR-38 lamps.

Furniture and art objects were carefully placed by the owners so recessed fixtures would provide light only where needed. Shown is a view of the living room.

Private terrace with loggia. The 1946 building was completely rebuilt except for two facades.

Master bedroom suite on the second floor. Recessed low-voltage luminaires highlight the fine quality furnishings.

Haddonstone Show Garden

Lighting Designer: John Cullen, Lighting Design, Ltd., London, England
Client: Mr. R. Barrow, Haddonstone, Ltd.
Project Location: Northampton, England
Award: 1983 IALD Award of Excellence

The 400-square-meter show garden presents Haddonstone Ltd.'s range of stonework columns and garden details in the setting for which they are intended. Every effort was made to conceal sources of illumination in order to focus complete attention on the architecture.

A variety of low-voltage fixtures was specially designed for the project. Balusters are downlighted from units developed to fit on the undersides of the balustrade rail. The columns and pool area are illuminated from small low-voltage spotlights mounted at the column tops. Urns are lit using discreetly-mounted PAR-36 narrow beam spotlights. Optical projectors illuminate the fountain on all four sides and frame it so exactly that no shadows are cast and a slightly surreal effect is created.

Hard-to-detect low-voltage spotlights are mounted at the top of the columns.

Specially-designed fixtures are concealed underneath the balustrade rail.

An unobtrusive PAR-36 narrow beam spotlight is focused on the urn.

CHAPTER 4 # MUSEUMS, INSTITUTIONS, AND PLACES OF WORSHIP

Presented in this chapter are facilities which the public or transitory groups are apt to use: galleries, places of worship, and institutional and governmental buildings.

Museums and Galleries

Basic considerations which help shape the lighting design for museums, galleries and exhibit spaces—and which are handled successfully by two featured gallery projects—include:

1. The lighting must illuminate objects well enough so that details and textures may be studied and appreciated by the viewer. Colors should be rendered clearly and not muddied by the light source. Copy panels should be displayed and lighted so they can be read easily. Glare, which can distract and tire eyes, should be avoided. In the Forbes Magazine Galleries, good color-rendering reflector lamps are used with framing projectors that control where the light falls.

2. Pacing of the lighting, as well as of the display design, should be varied enough to hold the viewer's interest, to avoid monotony, and to encourage movement through the exhibits. A popular technique, also used in the Forbes Galleries, is to use light on displays only to attract attention and to allow pathways to remain in shadow. In the DeWitt Wallace Gallery, the display and lighting techniques change from one section to another: from individually isolated cases, to larger special exhibits, to study spaces.

3. Light sources must be chosen which minimize or eliminate heat and ultraviolet that can cause fading of colors and deterioration of fabrics and other organic materials. In the DeWitt Gallery, for example, shielding has been installed to

protect pieces from ultraviolet. The use of sensors and control devices is beneficial, particularly in exhibits where delicate objects would suffer from subjection to constant illumination. Computer-timed dimmers in the DeWitt Gallery illuminate study cabinets for 90-second periods.

4. Since displays change periodically, a system incorporating flexibility and easy maintenance is desirable. Track systems—used in both projects—are among the most popular.

Places of Worship

One of the advantages of using light as a design tool is that the same or comparable mood and atmosphere can be created with a variety of approaches and techniques, working hand in hand with the architecture and interior design. Compare the two indoor places of worship. The soothing shadows of St. Anselm's Church are pierced by shafts of light from fixtures concealed along the right and left walls. In contrast to this play of light and shadow is the uniform illumination of the Sanctuary of the Shiga Sacred Garden. Both environments are relaxing and conducive to prayer and meditation, even though the lighting techniques and effects differ.

What both lighting designs have in common is the studied, careful response of the lighting to the architecture and interior. The feeling of coldness, usually associated with concrete, is avoided in St. Anselm's by allowing the warm, white light that grazes the roughened texture of the walls to direct attention to the simple splendor of the altar area. The extremely high and long Shiga Sanctuary could have looked cavernous and forboding. Instead, evenly illuminated, the curving, delicately-capped interior seems like a canopy, gently enclosing and protecting its inhabitants.

Institutions

Traditionally, many institutional and governmental spaces have been associated with bland colors, barely functional furnishings and seemingly minimal consideration for personal comfort and aesthetics. The projects here offer a break from "tradition."

Through the thoughtful planning of the designers, these installations avoid some of the common lighting problems which can make a space look shabby and carelessly designed. In the Palm House at Dowling College, for example, shadows on occupants' faces, usually caused by downlights, are avoided because the designers chose to use pole fixtures which incorporate light sources mounted at a low enough level to illuminate faces evenly. In the Jefferson County Courthouse, lamps are screened by a parallel-blade louver to prevent glare in the eyes of viewers looking down on these first-floor fixtures from the second floor.

These projects demonstrate that institutional and governmental, limited-budget facilities can be comfortable, attractive and reflect a positive image for the client.

Shrine to Daikoku-Sama

Lighting Designer: Motoko Ishii, Motoko Ishii Lighting Design, Tokyo, Japan
Architect: Masayoshi Itoh, Itoh Architects & Associates
Photographer: Yutaka Kono, Yutaka Kono Photo Office
Client: Shinji Shumei-Kai
Project Location: Shiga, Japan
Award: 1985 IALD Honorable Mention

Daikoku-Sama, one of seven lucky gods believed by the Japanese people to bring happiness and wealth, is revered in a shrine in the Sacred Garden of Shinji Shumei-kai. The Daikoku-Sama seems to float in the shadowless illumination produced by halogen spotlights, which also add sparkle to and reveal the texture of the back screen.

The inner chancel of the shrine is protected and enclosed by adjustable walls on four sides which, when lowered vertically into the ground, transform the chancel into an open and accessible space ready to be used for ceremonies. Seventy-nine incandescent ceiling-recessed lamps are placed where the walls meet the ceiling to serve as wallwashers when the chancel is enclosed, and to illuminate the floor, emphasizing the openness of the space, when the walls are withdrawn.

All the lighting fixtures are hidden from view to preserve the clean architectural lines and to avoid distracting visitors. The simple lighting plan achieves a subdued, solemn atmosphere suitable for worship.

Here the inner walls of the chancel have been recessed into the ground. The band of illumination in the ceiling complements the clean architectural lines. The halogen spotlights emphasize the three-dimensionality of the golden back screen.

Forbes Magazine Galleries

Exhibition and Lighting Designers: Peter Purpura and Gary Kisner, Purpura & Kisner, Inc., New York, NY

Photographer: Larry Stein, pp. 115, 116 top, 117; Peter Purpura, all others

Client: *Forbes* Magazine

Project Location: New York, NY

Award: 1985 GE Award of Distinction

The Forbes Magazine Collection was begun over 30 years ago, and portions were displayed for nearly 20 years in the lobby of the Forbes Building in midtown Manhattan. Mr. Forbes, wishing to display a larger selection of items, vacated the ground floor of the building and gave over 8,000-square-foot of space to showcase the collections of American Presidential manuscripts and related historical documents, jewelled Fabergé art objects, miniature rooms, toy boats and soldiers, trophies and paintings.

The designers responsible for the innovative, imaginative displays for the toy boats and soldiers, trophies and Fabergé also designed the lighting system. In all these exhibit areas, MR-16 lamps in cool-light and mini-cube fixtures are installed. The small, handsomely-styled units are appropriately scaled to complement the low ceilings. These flexible luminaires create dramatic pools of light that contribute to the varied pacing and the avoidance of monotony. The light source renders color well and is cool enough to eliminate the possibility of heat damage to art objects enclosed in glass cases. The long life of the lamp minimizes maintenance.

Framing projectors guide shafts of light onto copy panels and original artworks without distracting spill. Since only the accent illumination is reflected off the art objects, glare from ambient light is nonexistent.

The Toy Boats section features ocean liners, warships, riverboats, an occasional sailboat and even a tin-lithographed Noah's Ark. More than 500 craft, manufactured between 1870 and 1955, are displayed.

The first part of the Toy Soldier exhibition traces the development of small-scale figures, placed in imaginative settings, using examples from major manufacturers. In "The Land of the Counterpane," the visitor can see a Wild West shootout, review George Washington's troops and admire the ornate Coronation Coach of King George V.

The Fabergé objects stand out against soft pink and mauve backgrounds. The colors were the favorites of Czarina Alexandra, the first recipient of the jeweller Fabergé's famous ornate and precious Easter Eggs.

The Forbes Magazine Collection is one of the oldest corporate collections in America and one of the few permanently on public display. In spite of the enormous quantity of objects in the collection, the skillfully designed exhibits surprise, entertain and intrigue visitors.

(Historical information used in the text and captions on the Forbes Magazine Galleries was obtained from *Highlights from the Forbes Magazine Galleries*, by Margaret Kelly, Forbes, Inc., Publishers, New York, 1985.)

Because of low ceiling height, small, handsome fixtures using MR-16 lamps were chosen. Shown are portions of the "Victory at Sea" warships.

All the major manufacturers of the toy boats are
represented in the "Ships Ahoy" exhibit. The
golden age of toy boats ended in the 1950s,
when the favorite mode of transportation
changed from boats to planes, and the material
of which most toys were made changed from tin
to plastic.

New York harbor forms the backdrop for a display
of battleships in the rear and luxury ocean liners in
the foreground.

The light source renders colors clearly and vividly.

Shown are submarines and other beneath-the-sea craft. Interplays of light and shadow among the suspended toys and models create a playful illusion of the murky deep.

A variety of toy boats is displayed in the whimsical, old-fashioned bathtub setting, including: Art Deco speedboats and cast-iron boat banks on the shelf, cast-iron and tin pull-toy rowers on the bathtub ledge, and steam-powered boats on the floor at the left.

The beautiful items featured are made with nephrite, one of two varieties of jade, that was mined in Siberia. Shown are: Imperial Presentation Tray, Twenty-Fifth Anniversary Clock, Nicholas II nephrite box, laurel wreath swing frame, Hvidore seal, desk pad and pencil, Grand Duchess Olga paper knife, holly spray, clock, miniature watering can, miniature basket of lilies of the valley, and miniature drinking cup.

Czarina Alexandra's favorite colors, pink and mauve, are used as a soft backdrop for the Fabergé exhibit. Fabergé employed 500 craftsmen who produced the detailed jewelled treasures.

Objects enhanced by the artistry of Faberge include: tortoiseshell lorgnette, polar bear and elephant, easel and frame, "Snowflake" pendant with red cross, Nobel necklace, "ice" pendant, cigarette-holder egg, glue pot, ostrich-feather fan, white frame, cuff links, vodka charki, knitting needles, and card-suit ashtrays. These items are made and studded with gold, silver, diamonds, rubies, enamel, ebony, ivory, rock crystal, and platinum.

A silver paddle-steamer music box, that plays "God Save the Czar" and "Sailing Down the Volga," was presented to Czar Nicholas' son, Alexis, by the Volga Ship Builders in 1913.

The 12,000 toy soldiers displayed in the galleries are a portion of the over 100,000 warriors in the Forbes Collection. The majority are housed in the Forbes Museum of Military Miniatures in Tangier, Morocco.

The pools of light focus attention on the displays. No ambient illumination is necessary.

DeWitt Wallace
Decorative Arts Gallery

Lighting Designer: LeMar Terry, Terry, Chassman & Associates, New York, NY
Photographer: Colonial Williamsburg staff photographer
Exhibits Designer: Vincent Ciulla Design
Client: DeWitt Wallace Decorative Arts Gallery
Project Location: Williamsburg, VA
Award: 1985 GE Award of Distinction

The gallery houses the Colonial Williamsburg Foundation's collection of 17th and 18th century American and English decorative art. The underground facility is 62,000 square feet; 26,000 feet is exhibit space.

The exhibits are divided into three parts, each presenting a different viewpoint of the decorative arts, and each enhanced by a different lighting-created mood. The illumination is also planned to move visitors along from one space to the next and to maintain interest throughout.

In the first series of exhibits, each work of art is isolated and is displayed individually. A bright, cheerful atmosphere is produced by the combination of natural light, low-voltage track units, fluorescent SP35's and Q250 PAR-38 floodlamps. To prevent any damage to the pieces exhibited from ultraviolet rays, UF3 has been installed.

The second series of rooms presents special exhibitions drawn from the museum's collection. The inaugural exhibit, for example, was "Patron and Tradesman," and explored the relationship between those who use and those who make decorative objects. Since the exhibits change periodically, a flexible low-voltage system is used, which creates drama through highlighting and accenting.

The third area contains spaces where visitors can study objects grouped by medium. In the Metals Study area, floor to ceiling casework with flexible interiors is illuminated by MR-16 and 12-volt lamps. In the Textile Study space, large vertical racks can be moved by demonstrators to show visitors 20 to 30 artifacts in one viewing. Care was taken to devise illumination that would produce 8 candelas for the best viewing of and minimum damage to the fabrics. The MR-16 lamps, raking 12-volt floods and SP35 lamps in this section are fitted with filters, rather than dimmers, to produce good color rendering without any shifting to the red end of the spectrum.

Accessible study cabinets allow visitors to examine objects closely and in depth for a set time period. The MR-16 lamps, on special computer-timer dimmers, furnish an ambient glow. Accent lighting is provided by 12-volt and 5.5-volt PAR-36 lamps. The visitor activates these for 90 seconds of study cabinet viewing. The remainder of the time, lighting is kept at three candelas from 7TTK and 9TTK fluorescent luminaires.

The Furniture Study Gallery contains groupings of over 8,000 pieces, arranged by colonial region and lighted by appropriately angled track units. In the Flower Room, next to the furniture exhibits, Q250 PAR floods provide the necessary ultraviolet for the flourishing of orchids and other flowers.

A control system turns lighting on and off automatically to conserve energy and preserve art objects. Included in the lighting program for the gallery was the instruction of staff members on how to use the lighting instruments.

Adjustable track units are angled to draw attention to important aspects of the over 8,000 pieces in the Furniture Study Gallery.

Floor plan.

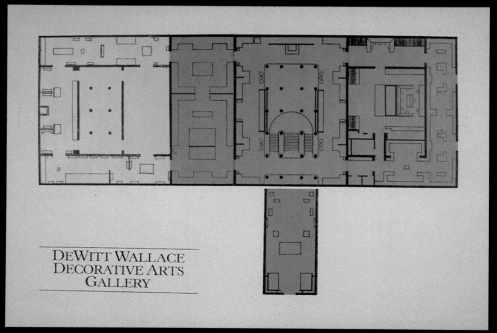

DeWitt Wallace
Decorative Arts
Gallery

An 18th century clothespress is "exploded" into its several parts and displayed near the original, assembled artifact to reveal complexity and craftsmanship of the piece. Low-voltage lighting is kept to a maximum of 10 candelas to protect the woods of the furniture.

Art objects are showcased and illuminated individually in the first series of exhibits.

The interiors of the casework in the Metals Study area are flexible. The high Kelvin temperature (which produces whiter light) of the MR-16 and 12-volt lamps enhance the glistening tones of the metals.

The visitor can pull out study cabinets from under the display cases and activate accent lighting, all at 8 candelas, for a 90-second examination period.

On the left can be seen the moveable, vertical textile racks, used to display 20 to 30 artifacts at a time. Illumination is at 8 candelas to protect the delicate fabrics.

The Palm House at Dowling College

Lighting Designer: Steven Mesh/Diana Juul
Architectural Lighting Design,
New York, NY
Architect: Nicholas Quennell;
Andrew Moore, project manager
Quennell/Rothschild
Associates
Photograhers: Steven Mesh for pp. 124–6,
128; all others © 1986
Laura Rosen
Client: Dowling College
Project Location: Long Island, NY
Award: 1986 IALD Honorable
Mention

The Palm House conservatory was built as part of a turn-of-the-century Vanderbilt mansion in Oakdale, Long Island. Today the mansion is occupied by Dowling College and houses classrooms and administration offices. The glass and cast iron Palm House, which connects two buildings and serves as the campus centerpiece, is approximately 32 feet high, 46 feet wide and 68 feet long. The space has no permanent furniture, because its function often changes. It is used as a student lounge, banquet room, lecture and concert hall and presentation room.

The lighting system had to be flexible enough to serve all the uses of the space, yet complement the lacelike glass and iron structure. A tight construction schedule and a restrictive budget had to be met.

The lighting system installed is three-fold:

1. Adjustable fixtures are mounted unobtrusively on track attached to the cast-iron ceiling structure. These units, which use 240 PAR-56 very narrow 12-volt spotlights, 300 PAR-56 NFL standard voltage, and 150 PAR-38 lamps are aimed to illuminate the floor, wall and podium.

2. Glass-globed street lights with 150 A-21's are positioned in the corners of the room. The pole fixtures provide a low enough source of light to illuminate occupants' faces evenly and to avoid shadows often caused by downlights. The light from the globes reflects off the few matte surfaces in the room—floor tiles, cast iron and window mullions. The style of the fixture fits in with the turn-of-the century architecture.

3. The old vent holes that encircle the room are filled with fixtures housing 25 T6½ CL's (showcase bulbs). The glowing perimeter, reflected in the glass wall and ceiling panels, adds a touch of elegance and sparkle to the room.

A preset dimming system allows untrained college personnel to select the appropriate combination of lighting levels and units for any function.

The room contains no permanent furniture because it is used for an ever-changing variety of functions.

One of the difficulties in developing a lighting scheme was the lack of reflective materials in the space and the abundance of glass, which appears dark when viewed from inside at night.

The ornate street poles provide a lower-height level of lighting that helps to humanize the scale of the large, high-ceilinged room.

The adjustable track can be seen mounted at the peak of the ceiling structure. The vent-hole fixtures encircle the room.

A view from the exterior reveals non-glaring, even
illumination with all three lighting systems activated.

At night, the room glows pleasantly when viewed from outside.

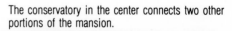
The conservatory in the center connects two other portions of the mansion.

Jefferson County Courthouse

Lighting Designer: Donald Gersztoff, Wheel Gersztoff Friedman Associates, Inc., New York, NY
Architect: The White Budd Van Ness Partnership, Beaumont, TX
Consulting Engineers: Galewsky and Johnston
Photographers: Robert Benson, p. 133; all others, Charles McGrath
Client: Jefferson County
Project Location: Beaumont, TX
Award: 1983 IALD Award of Excellence

The desired image of power and authority for the two-storey courthouse is embodied in strong architectural features which are reinforced simply, but boldly, by the lighting. By day, the central lobby and curved stairwell are illuminated by a vast skylight. By night, a sleek, tubular luminaire, which mimics the perimeter of the stairwell, provides illumination.

The polished, extruded aluminum tubing is suspended about 0.5m below the ceiling and houses 40-watt warm-white fluorescent lamps. Ballasts are hidden from view in the ceiling above. A continuous, baked-white enamel reflector directs light from the lamp through the 85-degree opening. The concentrated line of brightness on the ceiling echoes the luminaire's shape and the architectural line while providing required lighting levels.

To prevent disturbing glare in the eyes of visitors looking down from the second floor, the lamps are screened by a parallel-blade, matte-white finish louver. The opening of the tubular housing is rotated toward the interior wall at an angle of 12 degrees from the vertical.

Courtroom entrances, located on the long sides of the lobby, are highlighted by supplementary lighting from ceiling-recessed downlights housing 100-watt high-pressure mercury lamps. Inside the courtrooms, the circular theme of the lighting system is continued. Straight segments of the indirect tubular luminaires, also containing 40-W warm-white fluorescent lamps, are suspended in a circular array below the ceiling. The circle's center is equipped with five 40-W fluorescents shielded by a concave acrylic diffuser. A curved lighted cornice emphasizes the wood paneling of the entrance doors. The cost of operation is modest, and the maintenance is easy.

Rings of brightness reinforce both the architecture and the luminaire.

The luminaires contain 40-W warm-white fluorescent tubes and are hung from stainless steel cable.

136™ DISTRICT COURT

Courtroom entrances are emphasized by
ceiling-recessed downlights with 100-W high-pressure
mercury lamps.

CRIMINAL DISTRICT COURT

The circular theme is carried into the courtrooms.

Saint Anselm's Church

Lighting Designer: Motoko Ishii, Motoko Ishii Lighting Design, Tokyo, Japan
Architect: P.T. Morimura & Associates
Photographer: Motoko Ishii Lighting Design
Client: St. Anselm's Church
Project Location: Tokyo, Japan
Award: 1984 IES Edwin F. Guth Memorial Award of Excellence

The church, designed by the late Antonin Raymond and completed in 1954, was refurbished in 1983. Specifically, improved acoustics and new lighting for the sanctuary and baptismal hall were designed and installed.

A total of 16 floodlights (eight 250-watt halogen lamps on each side) are mounted 30 feet high to illuminate the sanctuary. The strong beams cutting across the concrete walls create interest and at the same time are angled to direct attention to the altar area. Two floodlights in the altar area (one on either side) are mounted at a lower level. The fixtures are fitted with black-painted revolving louvers to prevent glare.

Fourteen fixtures (seven on each side) are mounted on the lowered ceilings which run along the sides of the church. The units contain 100-W incandescent lamps and have a copper-plated finish to harmonize with the interior of the lobby. The baptismal hall is indirectly lit by fluorescent fixtures designed to emit a softer glow upward toward the ceiling.

All units, except fluorescent, are dimmer-controlled. Illumination levels are high enough to provide visitors with comfortable, non glaring reading light, while maintaining a relaxing, peaceful atmosphere conducive to prayer and meditation.

Piercing shafts of light angled downward graze the rough surface of the concrete walls and direct attention to the altar.

Sanctuary of the Shiga Sacred Garden

Lighting Designer: Motoko Ishii, Motoko Ishii Lighting Design, Tokyo, Japan
Architect: Ito Architects & Associates
Photographer: Akihisa Masuda, Japan Photographer's Committee
Client: Shinji Shumei-kai
Project Location: Kyoto, Japan
Award: 1984 IALD Honorable Mention

The large, awe-inspiring Sanctuary is 279 feet long, 184 feet wide and 127 feet high. The smooth, gently curving walls are crowned by a ceiling made luminous with concealed metal halide luminaires. Halogen downlights add glowing visual accents to the ceiling's delicate pattern, as well as provide even illumination to the floor below. Also housed in the ceiling are xenon and halogen spotlights that highlight the golden screen in the front of the Sanctuary.

Decorative chandeliers are used in other areas of the building to add elegance and interest to the neutral-colored, streamlined spaces. The first floor lobby features a stainless steel, half-mirrored, oval-shaped chandelier with a lacelike pattern. In the foyer, petal shapes etched in the beige ceiling come together in the center and are capped by a glistening circular chandelier.

Outside the Sanctuary, floodlights are focused on trees. Low footpath lights are used instead of poles so that the beauty of the natural setting surrounding the compound can be appreciated fully. For the Sanctuary plaza, 29½-foot-high polelights with stainless steel half-mirrored glass were designed. These form a complementary foreground for the nighttime-illuminated roof and marbled walls of the Sanctuary beyond.

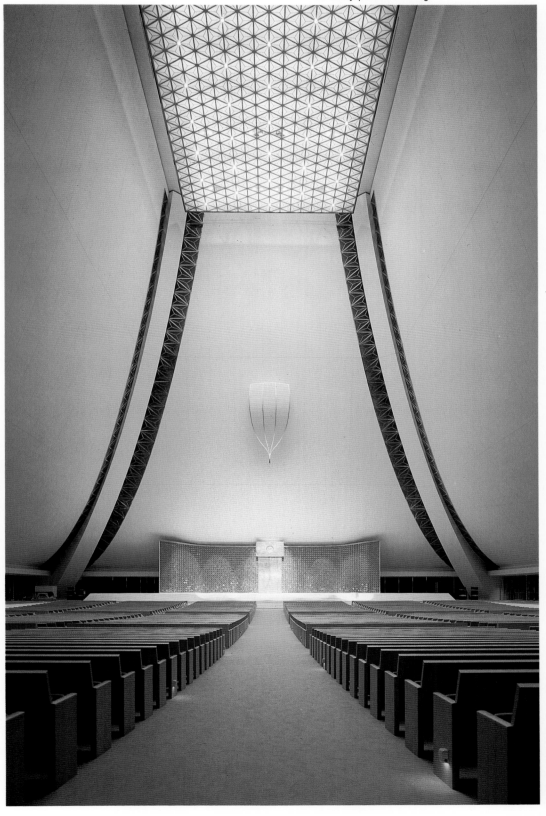

The high walls remain smooth and unblemished by lighting equipment which is concentrated in the delicately-patterned ceiling.

CHAPTER 5 RESIDENCES

Perhaps more in residential applications than in any other kind, a designer must be sensitive to the individual tastes of the client. It is the particular challenge of the residential designer to successfully blend the client's lifestyle and tastes with the range of space, budget, energy and environment limitations that apply in designing for other types of installations as well.

Interiors

In two projects featured here, each client wanted art collections highlighted by the lighting. Yet the resulting designs are very different. In Art Collections for a Private Home, this is accomplished simply and elegantly with recessed downlights. Very little of the occupant's attention is drawn to the lighting system so that maximum attention can be given to the art. In The Laboratory, on the other hand, not only are the artworks enhanced, but the light itself serves as art, as the client wished. The color washes, lasers and kinetic light effects are meant to be noticed by the occupant.

The Sawyer House is an example of how environment and climate can encourage the selection of one lighting technique over another. The sophisticated daylighting system, which "connects" the interior of the home with the natural beauty of the Rio Grande bosque outside, would be out of place or less effective in a bleaker or urbanized environment.

Sometimes energy availability is a primary influence of the design choice. The sumptuous Yacht Regina is fitted with low voltage neon and acrylic tubing because of limited power available from the on-board generator used when the yacht is at sea. Space and structural limitations played a part in the selection of a track system for Raphael Condominium—there was no ceiling space in which fixtures could be recessed.

Exteriors

Two trends are evident in the outdoor projects included here. First, there is a striving for sculptured effects—controlled beams of light are directed onto specific areas to outline, graze and focus on the details of an object or limited area—rather than broad and uniform floodlighting. Secondly, an effort has been made to conceal fixtures from view as much as possible.

The designer for Stonebridge Condominium developed his own low-profile, streamlined housing for a lamp most commonly used indoors—the MR-16—so that he could delicately spotlight waterfalls, outline plantings, and graze stonework outside a condominium complex. After considering and ruling out more commonly used floodlighting techniques, the lighting consultant for Four-Leaf Sculpture custom designed carefully concealed neon to intensely illuminate a 50-foot slit in a towering metal obelisk. With the aid of the latest in controls and dimmers, the designer for Japanese Garden Light composed well-balanced, etched scenes for an outdoor light show.

Sawyer House

Architects (responsible for daylighting design): Don Felts and Nancy Weinman, Don Felts, Architect, Albuquerque, NM

Photographers: Robert Reck Photography

Client: Robert and Catherine Cassidy Sawyer

Project Location: Albuquerque, NM

Award: 1985 IALD Award of Excellence

The private residence is located on two acres of flat land in the Rio Grande bosque. In this desert oasis, cottonwood forests, alfalfa fields, orchards and vineyards flourish. Because the views of the surrounding area are so beautiful—a river to the west, the Sandia Mountains to the east—the residence includes outdoor garden areas with walls that shield the occupants from immediate neighbors, but allow visual access to the distant mountains.

The beauty of the outdoors is brought into the home via a sophisticated skylight system that furnishes each room with washes of daylight from at least two directions. Each skylight contains an aluminum reflector/sunshade with a pan attached to curved tubular aluminum struts. Glass mirrors mounted on the front surface of the reflector pans substantially increase the skylight's solar and heat gain. During the summer, telescoping front struts allow the reflectors to be lowered to shade the skylights and to help cool the rooms.

All the major spaces have a system of south-facing reflector-equipped skylights, which make a striking architectural statement and glow at night with reflections of interior electric light.

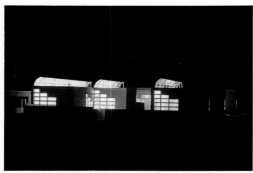

Radiant electric ceiling heating assists the passive solar heating system. Cooling is accomplished through night ventilation and evaporative coolers.

Section plan.

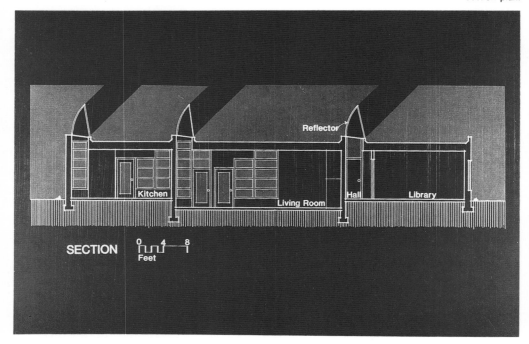

Reflector

Kitchen   Living Room   Hall   Library

SECTION   0   4   8
           Feet

The mirrors glow at night with reflections of interior light. Skylights are low iron glass in an aluminum frame.

The 2,800-square-foot wood frame house has a gypsum board finish for all north and south walls and for the roof. East and west walls are used for thermal storage and consist of masonry with the cores grouted solid and a plaster finish. The exterior is stucco.

Floor plan.

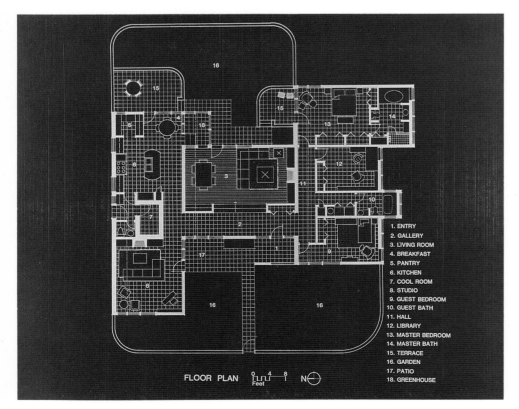

1. ENTRY
2. GALLERY
3. LIVING ROOM
4. BREAKFAST
5. PANTRY
6. KITCHEN
7. COOL ROOM
8. STUDIO
9. GUEST BEDROOM
10. GUEST BATH
11. HALL
12. LIBRARY
13. MASTER BEDROOM
14. MASTER BATH
15. TERRACE
16. GARDEN
17. PATIO
18. GREENHOUSE

FLOOR PLAN   0 4 8 Feet   N

In summer, the adjustable reflector/sunshades block the direct sun and keep the skylights in cool shade.

The combination of daylighting and electric lighting produces a pleasantly balanced luminous environment.

The concrete slab on grade floors has a tile finish in all rooms except the living room, which has maple sleepers over the concrete.

Since the two owners have diverse working hours, the living and sleeping areas are distinctly separated.

The Laboratory

Lighting Designer: Tully Weiss, Tully Weiss Lighting Design, Dallas, TX
Photographer: Doug Tomlinson, Doug Tomlinson Photography
Client: Anonymous
Project Location: Dallas, TX
Award: 1984 IES Edwin F. Guth Memorial Award of Excellence

Here is a designer's dream job: no energy restrictions and very little monetary stipulations. The residence is called "The Laboratory" by the client because of the unusual and creative approach to lighting the space. The goals were to facilitate the creation of varied moods, to enhance the art collection, to incorporate flexibility and to allow the light itself to be used as art.

To achieve the goals, 300 state-of-the-art aircraft, theatrical, television and architectural lighting instruments from France, Japan, Italy and the U.S. have been combined into a complex and sophisticated system. The highlight is a 2-watt argon laser. This is the only laser on record with the FDA for residential use and has been approved by that agency for use in this application.

The cost of the 3,200-square-foot project was $300,000. It uses over 75,000 watts. Shown are only a few of the many effects achievable using this lighting system.

The fun and game room atmosphere is reinforced by the bands of neon that run along the perimeter of the wall.

In the studio, 28 lighting instruments are installed on a custom batten system. An 18-channel, five-scene control is used. Neon can be dimmed.

The 9-foot, 6-inch painting greets the guest in the entryway, which is next to the dining room. Some fixtures are mounted on a custom batten.

The "daylight conversation setting," for reading and viewing of artwork uses 3½-inch and 4-inch ellipsoidals, 6-inch zoom ellipsoidals, PAR-36, -46, -56 and -64, line voltage 6, 12, 28 and low-voltage. Wattages range from 50 to 1,000 watts. Heat filters are used on high-voltage downlighting. Ultraviolet filters are used on all artwork. Temperatures range from 3200 degrees to 3400 degrees Kelvin.

Brilliant blue/green beams that scan the ceiling lines, wall-to-wall, are produced by the laser contacting an optical beam splitter. Light from this system is about two million times more concentrated than a 100-watt lamp. A beam expander is used for safety.

High-intensity beams in the living room are filtered very cool to complement the high-intensity blue laser crossing the ceiling. Yellow and green beams are split from the primary beam and directed in 90-degree and 45-degree angles. An odorless alcohol and water fog system with two-speed remote control is used in conjunction with laser effects and the house lighting system for definition of beam shape.

Automated x y mirrors create three-dimensional light sculptures composed of color washes. The high-speed scanner system varies the size of pattern, intensity and color. The laser washes the wall and floor and complements the living room artwork.

In the living room, a star-studded, romantic atmosphere is created by 1,000-square-feet of pencil-thin strands of physical light. Special ultraviolet is used for backlighting.

The "beam me up" effect relies on the high contrast of colors and shadows.

Crosslighting and high key lighting are used in the living room's "aggressive warm preset." The laser is scanning beyond the flicker rate of the eye and has created three different light tunnels, one blue and two green.

This preset enables the client to read comfortably from his bed (80-footcandle level) and to view the accented artwork.

In the bedroom, artwork is focused on with no distracting spill light. Colors are rendered vividly.

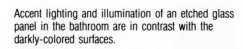

Accent lighting and illumination of an etched glass panel in the bathroom are in contrast with the darkly-colored surfaces.

Art Collections in a Private Residence

Lighting and Interior Designer: Tony Grant, ASID, Tony Grant, ASID, Design Corporation, Las Vegas, NV

Photographer: Patrick Bartek, Bartek Studios

Award: 1986 Halo/SPI National Lighting Competition First Place Winner

The interior spaces of this 5,000-square-foot residence are designed to be open and uncluttered. The simple line and form of the architecture is complemented by a simple, unobtrusive lighting system. Recessed incandescent downlights, wall sconces and conventional standing and table lamps minimize the attention paid by the occupant to the lighting and maximize the enjoyment of the rich materials used and the many pieces of artwork displayed.

A warm salmon, enriched by the incandescent sources, is the primary color used throughout the home, with balancing accents of black and aqua. In the dining room, medium-sized porcelain and metal art objects are displayed individually in square wall niches. Smaller objects are grouped on three levels of shelves contained within one large wall niche below. Accenting from recessed downlights makes them all sparkle and shine. The superb quality and reflective effect of the dining room and service area ceilings and walls was achieved through seven weeks of repeated plastering, sanding and spray painting.

In the living room, hand-painted Chinese silk covers the seating. Select red oak flooring has been bleached and stained to complement the custom-dyed carpeting. Golden bowl wall sconces at the entryways to the living and dining rooms counterbalance the straight lines of the interior architecture. Only one wall-covering—a vertically textured covering with a soft salmon hue—is used in the main areas of the first floor to unify the open spaces and maintain simplicity.

Conventional polished brass lamps and sconces provide appropriate illumination.

Architectural lines are clean and the rooms are uncluttered.

Incandescent downlights are used for all artwork displayed in the dining room.

Raphael Condominium

Lighting and Interior Designers: Alan Lucas, ASID, IBD and Jeffrey Werner, ASID, Alan Lucas + Associates, Inc., Mountain View, CA
Photographer: Mary E. Nichols
Client: Harold Raphael
Project Location: San Francisco, CA
Award: 1986 Halo/SPI National Lighting Competition 1st Place Award

The designer of the 408-square-foot, pie-shaped condominium produced a coherent yet varied lighting system in spite of the limitations of the space. Track lighting has been installed because of the extremely shallow ceiling recess. Low-voltage units, well-styled and scaled for the space, are positioned in a row in the hallway near the entry. Another track cuts diagonally across the living area. The MR-16 lamps allow interesting focal points to be established.

Laminate cabinets for storage are shaped in a triangular form in the living area. Soffits above them repeat the dynamic forms and create space for recessed lighting.

The space is enlarged visually through the use of mirrors and a limited palette of materials. The lighting brings a sense of drama to the architectural forms of the space by emphasizing textures.

Mirror walls make the space seem larger than it is. A diagonal strip of track runs across the ceiling of the living area.

Track lighting is used in the hallway. Recessed units focus on a corner display.

Lamps recessed in soffits light the small dining area.

Hyde Park Gardens

Lighting Designer: John Cullen, Lighting Design, Ltd., London, England
Architect: John R. Harris Architects
Interior Designer: Sami El Khazen, Sami El Khazen Interior Design
Client: Omar Aggad
Project Location: London, England
Award: 1983 IALD Honorable Mention

This 750-square-meter classical English home was completely refurbished. The illumination, like the interior design, combines traditional elements with modern techniques. This balanced blend is exemplified in the formal entrance halls. The open core of the circular stairwell is graced by an ornate, crystal chandelier. The high-domed ceiling is uplighted, and the arched niches in the stairwell walls are glowed by concealed strips of cold cathode.

The cold cathode continues into the living room across the coving formed by the tops of the pilasters and accentuates the arches. Tungsten-halogen uplights placed by the windows highlight the ornamental ceiling and provide a warmer light tone to the room. At the base of the window arches, beams from miniature recessed low-voltage units uplight to illuminate the undersides of the arches. Table lamps provide a local light source and balance the uplighting.

In the bar area, recessed low-voltage units are placed over the plantings and are spaced evenly around the curved wall of the bar to accentuate the polished wood paneling. General lighting and sparkle are provided by a custom-designed, two-tiered chandelier composed of a showering of silver and anodized brass chains with a large number of 10-watt, 6-volt lamps suspended at varying heights among the chains.

The totally white, master bedroom is softened by gold cone downlights. The richness of the silk draperies is revealed by miniature low-voltage pinspot downlights recessed close to the curtains. These downlights also create an interesting play of light and shadow on the shades.

The classical English home was refurbished to introduce the Middle Eastern cultural influence of the new owner.

Cold cathode accentuates the arched niches in the stairwell wall.

Concealed cold cathode also is used to highlight the dome visible from the entryway below.

Tungsten-halogen uplights accentuate the ornamental
ceiling in the living room.

The bar chandelier is composed of silver and anodized brass chains and 10-watt, 6-volt lamps.

Low-voltage pinspot downlights in the white master bedroom reveal the rich texture of the silk draperies and add interest to the window areas.

The Yacht Regina

Interior and Lighting Designer: Roy F. Sklarin, Roy F. Sklarin Interiors, Fort Lauderdale, FL

Client: Mr. and Mrs. Ernest Stern

Project Location: The clients are from Pittsburgh, PA. The Regina can be found frequently sailing the seven seas.

Award: 1984 IES Edwin F. Guth Memorial Award of Excellence

The owners of the 86-foot yacht, who had purchased it over 11 years earlier, wanted it completely custom-redesigned in a short time and at a reasonable cost. Although life aboard a yacht seems glamorous and exciting to most, there are restrictions and special conditions that are not concerns of the average on-land residential dweller. These limitations had a significant bearing on the design of the lighting system.

At sea, daytime brings an intense wash of sunlight and at night, a thick blanket of darkness. Though electrical power is abundant at dockside, at sea only a limited supply is available from an on-board generator, so usage must be carefully weighed. There is limited space to store or to conceal lighting equipment. Finally, the owner had requested that the lighting serve both as a functional element and as an aesthetic complement to the interior design.

The new exterior of the yacht—a pearl gray hull with recessed burgundy striping—set the tone for the interior. Inside, pearl gray flannel wall coverings complement carpeting that is also pearl gray with sculptured burgundy inserts. The color combination allows for high reflectivity of light without glare. The main salon is combined with the dining area to form an homogeneous 35 feet long and 22 feet wide space.

The designer chose to recess slender, custom-designed white neon tubing in a valance that runs along the perimeter of the salon/dining room ceiling. The neon's line of brightness accents the ceiling, makes the room seem more spacious, and adds a tonal variety to the wall coverings, which appear light gray nearest the light source, and progressively darker towards the floor. The low-voltage neon minimizes power usage, is a relatively cool source and has a long life.

Two etched glass panels, one on either side of the room, demarcate the dining room from the main salon. One panel depicts the yacht previously owned by the clients; the other, their current yacht, Regina. The panels are illuminated by fluorescent tubes built into the frames surrounding the glass. The glow highlights the etched details of the panels and the planters below. For easy maintenance and replacement of the light sources, a unique method of raising the frames has been devised.

A chandelier in the dining area is illuminated continuously for practical and aesthetic purposes. Its delicate points of brilliance contrast with the more even washes of the fluorescent panel units.

Incandescent and low-voltage acrylic tube lighting in both the chandelier and table lamps provide general illumination in the salon/dining area. This lighting has a guaranteed life of 15 years, and a low power draw. Stairwells are illuminated as well for safety.

In a bedroom, mirrored walls help to make the area look larger. Recessed incandescent downlights and small, wall-mounted reading lamps provide sufficient illumination without creating harsh or distracting glare.

The main salon connects with the dining room. The chandelier is left on continuously.

The designer reworked the original design to give the yacht a more European look, widening the salon to nearly 22 feet. The yacht looks like it is in motion even when it is standing still due to the angular design of the stern, bridge and windows and to the sleek, clean, burgundy accent lines.

In one of the bedrooms, recessed incandescent downlights and wall-mounted reading lamps provide glare-free illumination.

Illumination in the salon/dining area is from table lamps, a chandelier and valance-recessed neon tubing.

The Regina's interior cabinetry is custom-designed, as are many of the features in the functional galley. The craft can accommodate up to seven passengers and a crew of four. Shown is a portion of the main salon.

When the yacht is at sea, the interior is subject to intense sunlight by day and an unpierced blanket of darkness by night. The lighting for and colors of the interior take this into account.

This etched glass panel depicts the 100-foot classic motor yacht owned by the clients while the Regina underwent redesign. Fluorescent tubes surrounding the panel and hidden within a frame provide subtle illumination.

The Regina is etched in glass in one of two panels that divide the main salon from the dining area.

The white neon illumination runs around the perimeter of the salon/dining area. Here it can be seen through the etched glass panels. The sparkle of the chandelier adds interest to the dining area.

Stonebridge Condominiums

Lighting Designer: Bruce A. Kalkowski, MIES, B-K Lighting, Fresno, CA
Architect: Bill Fulton, Bill Fulton & Associates
Photographer: Alex Swiridoff, Swiridoff Photography
Client: William Irwin, Stonebridge Condominium
Project Location: Fresno, CA
Award: 1986 GE Award of Distinction

Although the condominium development was in varied phases of construction, it had to appear elegant, active and cohesive to visiting potential buyers. A favorable first impression greets the guest at the main entry, where the circle drive is adorned on either side by ponds, waterfalls, shrubbery and other well-kept plantings. It was the designer's task to extend the finished look of the entryway for nighttime viewing via the lighting.

The PAR lamp, normally specified for exterior floodlighting, did not provide the control and more delicate beam pattern that the designer envisioned. Also, the bulky, unattractive housing would detract from the beauty of the setting.

Instead, the MR-16 tungsten halogen lamp was chosen because of its excellent color rendering, compact size and beam control. No outdoor housing for the lamp existed, because the MR-16 is used mainly in interiors, but that did not stop the designer—he invented one.

The small, inconspicuous fixture, which is hidden easily in the foliage, is designed to withstand and protect the fragile lamp from harsh weather. There is no unwanted spill light, and glare is minimized.

By careful placement of the units, the lip of a waterfall is highlighted, a wall is grazed to reveal depth and texture, and with the addition of honeycomb baffles, signage is evenly illuminated. The intensity of the beam makes the flowing water appear brilliant and sparkling. The plantings seem to come alive with vivid color.

The project uses 1150 watts, three to four times less than would have been used with standard floodlighting equipment. The 12-volt lamps are safe near water, and no special safety precautions had to be paid for by the owner.

The intensity of the MR16 beam makes the water look bright white.

The entryway had to appear elegant to guests even though the project was still in a construction phase.

Note the lack of glare and spill light.

The good control of the light rendered by the fixture
allowed the designer to focus on the lip of a waterfall.

Japanese Garden Light

Lighting Designer: Kaoru Mende, TL Yamagiwa Laboratory Inc., Tokyo, Japan
Photographer: Toshio Kaneko
Landscaper: Ishikawa Zoen
Client: Nitto Tochi, Ltd.
Project Location: Japan
Award: 1985 IES Edwin F. Guth Memorial Award of Excellence

"A Japanese garden," in the words of the designer, "is a space that is the consolidation of traditional Japanese aesthetic senses. Unlike the geometric and artificial construction of western gardens, the construction of a Japanese garden reflects the spiritual attitude of the Japanese people to harmonize with nature." The promotion of harmony with nature is an integral part of the planning of the lighting design.

The garden outside the guest house is lighted so that it can be enjoyed by guests at night. The external garden is closely related to the interior by choosing the best illuminated settings possible as viewed from inside each room of the house. The lighting can be selected to correspond to whatever activity is taking place in the rooms of the house. For example, when dining in the second floor dining room, or when partaking in a tea ceremony on the first floor, the most beautiful lighting of the garden to be seen from that room can be displayed.

Also, a light show lasting eight minutes and composed of nine well-balanced scenes can be held with a 10-to-30-second fade time per scene. Built into the lighting control device is an eight-section circuit with dimmers. Each scene also can be selected by operating buttons on a wall panel in each room.

All fixtures are camouflaged with shrubbery and have been focused carefully. Color temperatures between incandescent for near foliage and mercury-vapor for distant landscapes are used accordingly. A traditional gardener was consulted and on-site tests were made to insure that lighting levels were in keeping with the peaceful and relaxing atmosphere of the garden.

The eight-minute light show is computer controlled. A traditional gardener was consulted on the appropriateness of the lighting levels.

The appreciation of the exterior garden from within the house is referred to as "Shakkei," which means "to borrow a landscape." As Japanese people view a garden, they celebrate the everyday changes of nature in poems and enjoy conversation about the subject.

Shown are some of the varied scenes of the landscape produced by the changing natural and planned electric illumination. Fixtures are well concealed in the shrubbery.

Four-Leaf Sculpture

Lighting Designer: Marlene Lee, PE, Marlene Lee Lighting Design/Consulting Engineers, San Francisco, CA
Sculptress: Beverly Pepper
Client: Gorgio Borlenghi, Interfin Corporation
Project Location: Houston, TX
Award: 1984 IES Edwin F. Guth Memorial Award of Excellence

A 60-foot obelisk cast of ductile iron stands in the entry plaza between the two towers of Four-Leaf Condominiums. A slot begins 10 feet above its base and runs to the tip. The sculpture rests on a 120-foot diameter flat disk, evenly overlaid with low, dense groundcover. The artwork was to be illuminated at night for the enjoyment of both residents and visitors.

Traditional floodlighting techniques were ruled out for several reasons:

1. The low reflectivity of the darkly-colored metal.

2. Bulky floodlighting fixtures would have marred the surrounding flat, open landscape.

3. Any floodlights directed upward would have produced disturbing glare in the eyes of anyone viewing the sculpture from the apartments.

The chosen solution was to light the slot from within, making the obelisk appear at night to be a "negative" rendering of its daytime "positive" image. The intense light within the sculpture comes from neon lamps mounted on both sides of the slot. The lamps are concealed cleverly by corten closure strips in 10-foot lengths shaped into a "U". The strips produce maximum reflectivity and are hinged for easy installation and maintenance. The strips also protect the transformers, lamp sockets and wiring that are attached to them.

The concentrated, well-controlled line of light narrows and widens as one views the sculpture from a variety of angles.

The sculpture stands between the two residential buildings.

There is no spill light to blemish the clean-lined sculpture or the surrounding environment.

Any fixtures mounted on the flat planar pad surrounding the obelisk would have been distracting and intrusive.

The illumination chosen is not glaring to condominium dwellers and their guests.

CHAPTER 6 OUTDOOR LIGHTING

Two popular approaches used in lighting building exteriors are:

1. To carry out the architect's intent by allowing the building to appear at night the way it looks during the day. This technique is used in the lighting of the RCA Building at Rockefeller Center. Light from specifically targetted, multi-vapor lamps mingles with shadows and plays upon the graduated planes of the building as sunlight would.

2. To decorate the exterior of the building with light, highlighting some architectural details and not others, to produce a totally different effect at night than is rendered in daylight. The exterior of the Platz Ohizumi shopping center is adorned with rows of continuous specially-designed fluorescent tubes in four different colors.

The use of color in exterior lighting helps to create a festive atmosphere. Lighting consultant, Douglas Leigh, has made "color with meaning" popular on buildings such as the Empire State Building in New York City. The building's tower changes color in accordance with the seasons, special occasions, or in honor of visiting dignitaries. Included in this chapter is the Electric Power Pavilion from the Tsukuba Expo '85. The white peaks of the tentlike roof are bathed at night in changing colors of red and blue, which symbolize steam power and water power, respectively.

Now that the energy crisis has abated, utilities have begun to join with manufacturers and lighting organizations in promoting programs to encourage exterior lighting of buildings. Building owners are also beginning to value both the positive, attention-getting image and the increased patronage that may result from nighttime exterior lighting of their establishments.

Luminaires which offer glare and beam control and sufficient intensity for longer throws of light have made it possible for designers to produce more sculptured effects and delicate highlighting of details. Long lamp life and computer controls have made maintenance and system operation easier.

A unique blending of the myriad of outdoor lighting effects is presented in the EPCOT Center project. The designer had to meet safety, maintenance and operational requirements, while at the same time bring an illusory, larger-than-life excitement and drama to the "theatrical set" of the ten EPCOT pavilions.

Rockefeller Center

Lighting Designer: Abe Feber, principal, and Aaron Chestnut, associate, Lighting By Feder, New York, NY

Primary Contractor: Ray DeGraw, Project Manager, L.K. Comstock & Co., Inc.

Electrical Engineers: Dominic Barradi, Project Manager, Edwards & Zuck

Structural Engineers: Edwards & Hjorth

Structural Framing: Northeastern Steel Fabricators

Roofing: E.O Osman

Photographers: G.R. Roston, photo on p. 190/191; Bo Parker. p. 185; Bart Barlow, p. 188; Michael N. Paras, all others

Client: Dennis Rehn, project manager, Rockefeller Center Management Corporation

Project Location: New York, NY

Award: 1986 City Club of New York Bard Award

The night visitor to the Rockefeller Center complex experiences a sense of grandeur, festiveness and emotional uplift due in large part to the spectacular lighting. The capstone of the project is the 850-foot, 70-storey RCA Building.

The lighting designer achieves at night the design intent architect Raymond Hood meant the building to have in the daytime. Light and shadow play upon graduated planes to create the illusion that the limestone tower is thinner and soars higher than it really is.

This is the only building in New York City illuminated completely from top to bottom. Because the complex is built like a miniature city-within-a-city, the designer was able to install the fixtures on the roofs and setbacks of the lower buildings clustered around the RCA tower. From 11 vantage points on 10 rooftops, multi-vapor luminaires mounted in steel racks direct patterns of targetted and controlled beams onto specific portions of the building. The effect is the sculpturing and accenting of architectural detail on the waterfall-like facades. For example, shafts from the fixtures mounted on the British Empire and La Maison Française buildings bathe the center shaft of the east facade. Lights on the International Building and One Rockefeller Plaza are directed to the uppermost section. The summit is encircled with 28 1,000-watt high-pressure sodium luminaires color-filtered to blend with the "RCA" red neon sign.

The tower fixtures are on one hookup circuited to a master computer on time clocks. Each independent targetted bank of fixtures is controlled by a master panel.

Complementing the magnificent lighted tower at ground level is the "umbrella of light" that graces the Promenade, Channel Gardens and Lower Plaza, also created with multi-vapor lamps. Two tonal values achieved with color filters are used in the sunken well/lower plaza area: one for summer, when the sunken well is used as an outdoor restaurant; one for winter, when it becomes an ice skating rink.

Two kinds of small, more compact multi-vapor lamps were developed by the designer and engineered by the manufacturer for this project. These are a 1,500-watt lamp (160,000 lumens) housed in a specially-designed mirrored searchlight and a 400-watt PAR-64 (36,000 lumens) housed in an existing fixture that was redesigned for the project. A total of 342 luminaires are used. The computer-controlled illumination is on from dusk to 1 A.M. each day.

Light test for the RCA tower. The tower is the only skyscraper in New York City illuminated from top to bottom.

The striking illumination sets the tower and Promenade/Channel Gardens area apart from the surrounding environment.

Lighting test for the RCA tower. This is one of
ten rooftops on which luminaires are mounted.

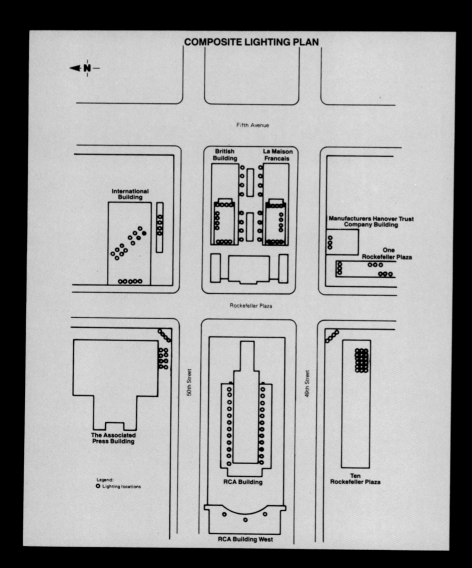

The kind of play of light and shadow produced
by sunlight is mimicked in the nighttime
rendering of the RCA tower.

The cool, twilight color of the forecourt and sculpture lighting is enhanced by its contrast with the warmer cast of the International Building interior behind it. This warm cast in the lobby is created through the highlighting of a 60-foot high copper-leaf ceiling and gold-leaf window-niche sculptures by high-pressure sodium luminaires.

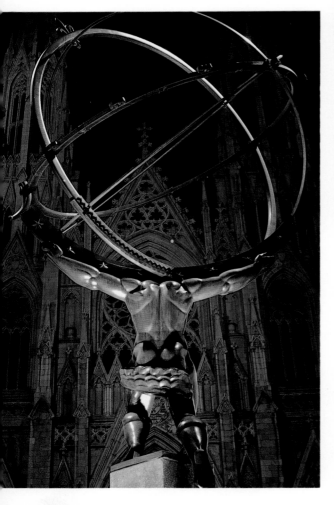

The multi-million dollar, multi-year enhancement program for the Rockefeller Center office, shopping and entertainment complex — of which the relighting of the RCA tower and Promenade areas is a part — is still in progress. The most recent addition is the lighting of the Atlas sculpture, and the lobby of the International Building which is situated behind the sculpture, completed in December 1986.

The "city within a city" design of the Rockefeller Center complex is reinforced by its new illumination. The brightness of the uniform washes of light creates an atmosphere of festiveness and excitement in contrast with the more subdued lighting of the city streets surrounding the center.

The unveiling of new lighting for Rockefeller Center coincided with the annual lighting of the giant Christmas tree traditionally placed in front of the RCA building. The switches were thrown on December 3, 1984.

The RCA tower viewed from several streets away.
Most of the building is lighted with multi-vapor
lamps. Ths summit is surrounded by a crown of
high-pressure sodium luminaires.

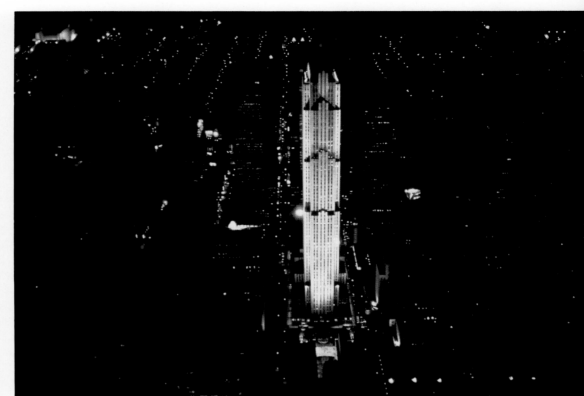

Shadows outline the details of the RCA Building's setbacks.

The lighting emphasizes the height of the structure.

EPCOT Center —
World Showcase Pavilions

Lighting Designer: Imero Fiorentino, Imero Fiorentino Associates, New York, NY
Architect: Walt Disney Imagineering
Photographer: Peter Crawford, Imero Fiorentino Associates
Client: Walt Disney World Co.
Project Location: Orlando, FL
Award: 1983 IES Edwin F. Guth Memorial Award of Excellence

On October 1, 1982, Walt Disney World opened the doors to EPCOT (Experimental Prototype Community of Tomorrow) Center, a 260-acre permanent World's Fair, located two miles south of Disney World in Orlando, Florida. It is the largest private construction project in history.

EPCOT is comprised of two distinct areas: Future World, where guests experience the technologies of tomorrow; and the World Showcase, which includes ten international pavilions (Canada, United Kingdom, France, Japan, American Adventure, Italy, Germany, China, Morocco and Mexico), set along the banks of the World Showcase Lagoon, where visitors experience a sampling of each country's culture, architecture and atmosphere. The lighting designer was responsible for the ten pavilions as well as the parade routes, promenade and lagoon islands.

Stage lighting depends greatly on the delicate balance between scenic and lighting elements to create a pleasant, effective picture. When this principle is applied to the lighting of buildings, and then to ten entire pavilions that are not under controlled conditions, it becomes a monumental task. Following are a few of the designer's goals and how he achieved them:

Goal: The lighting had to enhance the perspective and scale of the showcase as it is viewed from across the lagoon.

Solution: The roof lines, elevated architecture and natural forms are accented against the night sky so that each pavilion's identifiable features could be recognized even from a distance.

Goal: Walt Disney strongly believed that a theme park should always be reassuring. The street and garden lighting had to make visitors feel safe and confident as they explored the park at night. The equipment also had to complement the style of each pavilion and not interfere with the visitor's ability to see and appreciate the illuminated buildings above and around the streetlights.

Solution: The designer modified a fixture to contain two light sources. The "fake" source is a low-wattage, non-glaring lamp visible to the passerby. The "real" source that supplies most of the illumination is concealed in the fixture cap or base, and directs light onto the street and away from the eyes of visitors.

Goal: An important objective was to disguise or hide luminaires as much as possible.

Solution: For landscaped areas, a special small, thin, movable fixture was developed by the designer which is virtually camouflaged in the greenery. With high output, it is utilized to downlight flowers and shrubbery and to wallwash for foliage silhouettes.

In many of the pavilions, designers took advantage of architectural features to conceal fixtures. For example, pairs of serpent heads on the Mexican Pavilion's three pyramid facades incorporate recessed spot fixtures to light each other in a vertical progression up to the top. The visitor would find it difficult to locate more than just a few of the 4,800 fixtures used for the lighting of the World Showcase pavilions.

Although the architecture of the structures in the World Showcase uses past and present cultural style elements drawn from the "real world," the pavilions are not ordinary, solely functional buildings. They are illusion, magic, an enhancement and exaggeration of the real world. They are one huge, exciting theatrical set. The lighting, intentionally dramatic, imaginative, festive and theatrical, succeeds in allowing the visitor to "see the world" safely and stylishly by night.

Roof lines and elevated architectural forms are highlighted against the night sky so that each pavilion can be identified from across the lagoon.

The ceiling structure of the Japanese Pavilion is lighted by specially designed luminaires.

Surrounding the United Kingdom Pavilion are unique street lamps designed with concealed "real" light sources encased in the caps. Left is a daytime view. Shown above is the nighttime transformation.

The majesty of the formal fountain at the France
Pavilion is complemented by the subtle lighting of the
buildings' upper storeys and the Eiffel Tower in the
background.

At the Main Plaza of the United Kingdom Pavilion, light outlines roof structures and building crenelations. Sidewalk and street surfaces are illuminated from shop windows and archways.

Lighting units for the Mexico Pavilion are integrated into and highlight the ornamental design of the architecture.

At the entrance to the Japan Pavilion's Imperial Palace, overall balance is achieved through light level imbalance and variance on structural planes.

At the Germany Pavilion, form and depth are revealed through a mixture of light sources located inside and outside the buildings.

Here is a daytime view of the Germany Pavilion. The photo above shows its nighttime transformation.

The Cynara's Bridge and Floating Pier

Lighting Designer: Motoko Ishii, Motoko Ishii Lighting Design, Tokyo, Japan
Photographer: Yasuhiro Shimizu
Client: Cynara
Project Location: Misaki, Japan
Award: 1986 IALD Honorable Mention

In England (1927) the yacht Cynara was built. Over the years it has been enjoyed by several dignitaries, including Winston Churchill. Today, it is used for sightseeing and social functions. It is moored at a floating pier in the harbor of Misaki, a coastal town 32 miles south of Tokyo. The pier is connected to a long bridge that reaches across the water.

Ship lights line the bridge on either side at foot level and provide a sense of direction. The low positioning eliminates glare in the eyes of passengers and does not obstruct the view of the harbor beyond.

Four garden fixtures on low bollards are placed at even intervals to mimic the regularly-spaced floor-level lights. Mini-lamps attached to the underside of the bridge create the impression that the pier is floating on the water.

On the posts of the pontoon, halogen lamps are mounted which illuminate the Cynara and provide a bright, festive backdrop for the parties and social events taking place below. The awards jury praised the simplicity and consistency of the lighting design solution.

The pier seems to float on a shimmering pool of light.

Foot-level ship lights are placed at regular intervals on the bridge.

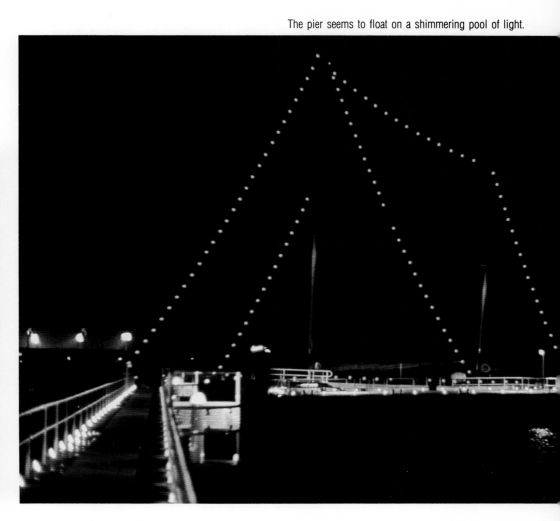

Electric Power Pavilion of Tsukuba Expo '85

Lighting Designer: Motoko Ishii, Motoko Ishii Lighting Design, Tokyo, Japan

Architect: Kisho Kurokawa, Kisho Kurokawa Architect & Associates

Photographer: Toshiharu Kitajima, p. 202 top, p. 203

Client: The Federation of Electric Power Companies

Project Location: Tsukuba, Japan

Award: 1986 IES Edwin F. Guth Memorial Award of Excellence

"Man, Environment and Technology" was the theme carried throughout the myriad of pavilions (60 foreign) of the third Japanese international exposition held in 1985 in Tsukuba, a university city 100 kilometers from Tokyo. The Electric Power Pavilion, sponsored by nine major Japanese power companies, was designed to attract young people's attention to the energy field.

In the design of the pavilion and its outdoor lighting, form and color were used to represent the types of energy offered by nature. The white peaks of the tentlike roof represent solar power and at night are bathed with changing colors of red and blue, which symbolize steam power and water power, respectively.

The color and intensity changes are unpredictable and exciting, because they are accomplished using the fluctuating power of the wind. One hundred seventy 500-watt floodlights are each fitted with two color revolving filters (red and blue). One is rotated by a breeze, the other by a strong wind. The effects vary depending upon the strength and direction of the wind.

This was the first time color floodlighting had been used with a natural source of energy supply. Floodlighting was also used to highlight a 98-foot steel tower in the pavilion's courtyard. Stroboscopic lighting was used on the exterior walls.

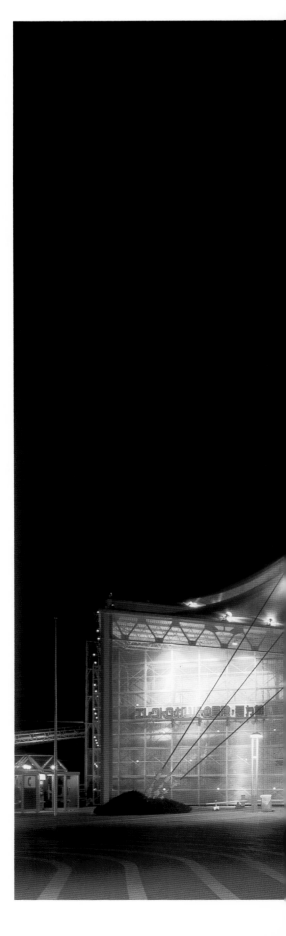

The floodlighted peaks of the Electric Power Pavilion point toward the 98-foot tower in the courtyard.

The interplay of primary colors comes from a super argon laser.

The designer also was responsible for a laser performance which took place atop the tower of the theme pavilion for the Japanese government.

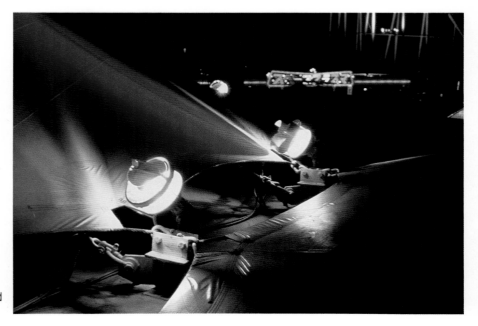

Lamps at the base of the peaks are fitted with red and blue filters.

Platz Ohizumi

Lighting Designer: Motoko Ishii, Motoko Ishii Lighting Design, Tokyo, Japan
Architect: Sakakura Associates
Photographer: Motoko Ishii Lighting Design
Client: Seiyu Co.
Project Location: Tokyo, Japan
Award: 1984 IES Edwin F. Guth Memorial Award of Excellence

Exterior illumination visually expresses the future-oriented approach of the six-level (five storeys, plus one basement level) shopping center. A canopied, see-through escalator adorned with colored ribbons of light is the outdoor focal point. The light-ribbons are composed of continuous rows of slim line 350-volt, ⅜-inch diameter fluorescent tubes, developed especially for the project by the designer and manufacturer. They run through the sales areas inside the building, as well as through the exterior escalator.

Four theme colors are used in varying combinations. Inside the main entrance on the first floor, six light lines curve and branch off into different sales areas. As the light lines wind upward in the escalator on the outside, the number of lines and colors decrease as they also branch off on each successive storey.

The high lighting level achieved by the slim lines eliminates the need for any supplementary lighting in the escalator. The lamps bend easily and are highly efficient. A total of 429 slim lines (2,160 feet) are used. The 300-hour life facilitates maintenance.

The exterior lighting is appreciated at night by patrons of the restaurants on the fifth floor which remain open until 10 P.M. Outdoor light poles surrounding the center are equipped with bands of neon to complement the building's exterior lighting scheme.

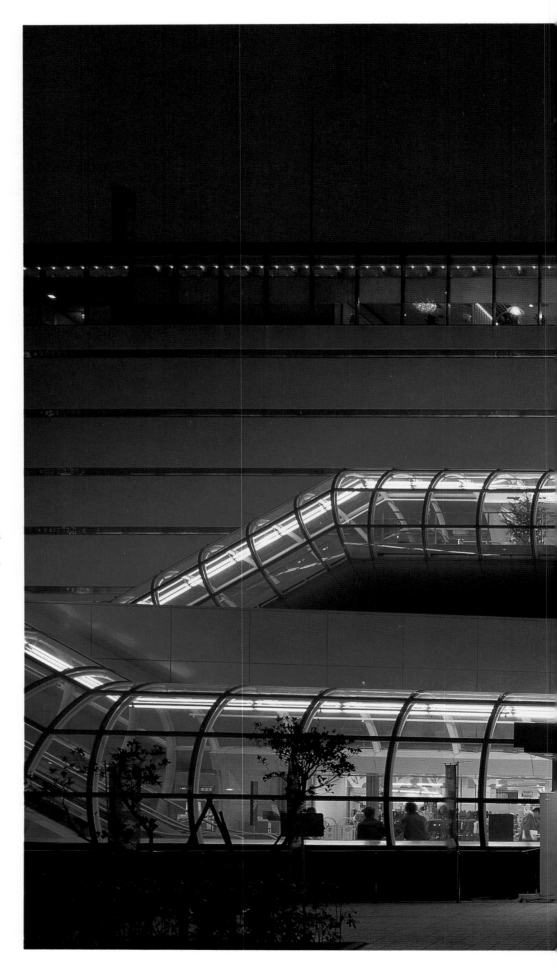

Bundles of slim line lamps illuminate the outdoor escalator that runs up to the fifth storey of the shopping center.

CHAPTER 7

IDEAS AND TECHNOLOGY FOR THE FUTURE

The seeds of the future are in the present. The way light is perceived and used today provides clues to where the lighting industry will be tomorrow. The four projects in this chapter embody state-of-the-art concepts and technology which most likely will influence the future of lighting.

Light as art is a relatively new phenomenon, and light artists have been gaining more widespread recognition since the 1970s. Light art can stimulate awareness and understanding of the qualities of light. The practicing consultant and the light artist have this in common: both can use the cold, high-tech, unfeeling, metal and glass tools of illumination to create beauty, warmth, richness in color, visual unity and emotion.

Abe Feder states in the Foreword: "Understanding how light and color affect emotion is also a significant factor in being a good lighting designer." As Eric Staller says of his Lightmobile, "This art comes to them (the viewers) and demands nothing except that they feel good." Light as art will probably continue to elicit recognition from the lighting design community because it keeps us in touch with the qualities of light that affect us emotionally and stir the imagination.

In speaking of the future, Abe Feder also states, "Soon there will be lasers, fiber optics, other forms of creating lighting energy and systems which will permit the designer a different palette of color, brilliance and tools with which to work." New light sources will be developed in decades to come, and new applications will emerge for sources which now exist in their developmental infancy. In the Laser Performance for the Sensazai, laser beams are split, reshaped and projected into varied patterns and designs to serve as an expression of religious symbolism. Lasers are used currently in such diverse fields as entertainment—in discos, theater events, outdoor exhibitions—and medicine—in surgery and medical treatments. But the laser as a resource is far from fully tapped, just as holography and fiber optics are only beginning to find new applications. These tools and others, used today by only a few, may be the common lighting tools of the future, bringing with them a changed perspective on design techniques.

In addition to new forms of light sources, there will be new sources of energy for producing light. A harbinger of this is the Civil/Mineral Engineering Building at the University of Minnesota, which uses passive and active solar systems to provide a portion of the lighting. The architect, David Bennett, states that in the future, the active solar system, "may perhaps be designed to operate at night with an intense electric source—a xenon arc lamp, for example—for a fraction of what it would cost to use a standard fluorescent."

This is one of many projects around the country that experiments with engineering techniques that draw on the natural resources and climate of the area in which the building is constructed. Research is being conducted to ascertain the effects of daylight and electric light on people physically and psychologically. Answers to these questions may influence what kinds of light we live and work under and what resources can be used to power them.

A driving force behind the development of new lamps, fixtures and sources of energy is the computer. Computers have pervaded every area of the lighting field: they are used to control the effects of

lighting systems; to aid in design and drafting; to perform calculations, measurements, fixture and lamp testing and design; and to render brightness levels within a space. In the Statue of Liberty project, though the computer was used throughout several phases of design development, perhaps the most astonishing computer contribution was the color simulation or modelling which depicted how the three-dimensional statue would appear when shaded or highlighted using a variety of

luminaires in varying positions. Far from replacing designers, the computer could free the designer from mundane and tedious tasks and leave more time for devising specific and customized solutions to design problems which would serve the client better and create more pleasant and productive environments for people.

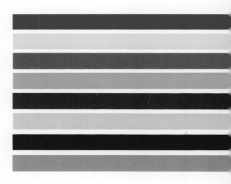

The Senzasai at Shiga Sacred Garden

Lighting Designer: Motoko Ishii, Motoko Ishii Lighting Design, Tokyo, Japan
Photographer: Motoko Ishii Lighting Design
Client: Shinji Shumei-kai
Project Location: Kyoto, Japan
Award: 1985 IES Edwin F. Guth Memorial Award of Excellence

The Senzasai is a religious event that involves the moving of the body of a god into a newly constructed house of worship. The Shumei-kai, a religious organization of the Shinto sect, held the ceremony at the Shiga Sacred Garden, nestled in the mountains, on May 1, 1983.

The performance took place at night in the outdoor plaza and inside the sanctuary building. It was divided into three parts:

1. The Prologue was held in the plaza. The directions of the moon and stars were pointed out by still laser beams. The Shumei-kai's organizational symbol was cast in the clouds above the roof of the sanctuary.

2. The Main Part of the performance was held in the sanctuary. Changing and colorful patterns of pure laser light, coordinated with organ music, danced upon the walls. Images symbolizing the

universe, time and man were intertwined and suggested the 21st century.

3. The Epilogue was performed outdoors, where the spectators and the plaza were wrapped in varied "cats cradle" plays of beams.

A 4-watt argon laser was used for the outdoor segments. A 4-watt argon and a 50-milliwatt helium neon laser were used inside the sanctuary. The purity of the wavelength and the intensity of the single, controlled beam create a magnificent light art.

A 4-watt argon laser was used in the outdoor plaza. During the Epilogue, the beams were split and reflected on the plaza.

The symbol of the Shumei-kai is etched by beams in
the clouds above the sanctuary building.

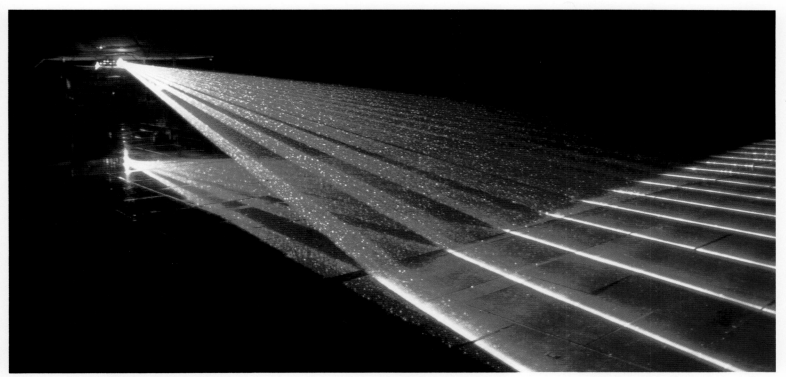

The laser beams are reflected on the plaza ground.

Beams radiate from the plaza to the sanctuary.

Lightmobile

Lighting Designer: Eric Staller, Artist, New York, NY
Engineer: Fred Niklas
Client: Eric Staller
Project Location: New York, NY
Award: 1986 IES Edwin F. Guth Memorial Special Citation

The light artist states, "I wanted to make something extraordinary out of something ordinary." The Volkswagen "beetle" was chosen as the basis for the artwork because it is unpretentious, whimsical and a form recognizeable to the common man.

The 1967 Volkswagen shell is perforated with 1,659 ¾-inch holes. Within the holes are tiny light sockets that are wired behind the sheet metal to a computer which can make the lights dance and change in an instant into 23 different patterns. The car's round form complements the rolling motion of the lights.

What is the effect of the mobile artwork on viewers? The artist has driven it in New York City and notes, "Smiles are universal and automatic, followed by shouts of thanks, applause, thumbs up." Many of the people who see it "have never been to a gallery or museum. Others feel excluded from modern art because they don't understand it. This art comes to them and demands nothing except that they feel good."

The impish curves of the car and rolling motion of the lights is in contrast with the imposing, angular and static skyscrapers of New York City.

University of Minnesota, Civil and Mineral Engineering Building

Architect: David J. Bennett, AIA, Bennett, Ringrose, Wolsfeld, Jarvis, Gardner, Inc., Minneapolis, MN
Client: University of Minnesota
Project Location: Minneapolis, MN
Award: 1984 IES Edwin F. Guth Memorial Special Citation

The Civil and Mineral Engineering Building is mandated by the state to be a demonstration project for the latest techniques in energy usage and earth-sheltered design. The bulk of the building is 110 feet below ground. Of that, 35 percent is in space mined below bedrock.

The building serves as a gateway to the Institute of Technology beyond—a complex comprised of seven buildings. The design of the CME Building took into consideration site utilities, solar access and shadow patterns from adjacent structures. Two kinds of daylighting systems are incorporated: active and passive.

The passive solar system brings daylight to the huge main structural lab, housed in the portion of the building that rises 50 feet above ground and that is clad in oversized brick to match surrounding structures. A giant, orange-painted, steel truss supports a 15-ton traveling crane that is used to transport large items into the structural lab for study and testing.

The passive solar system, mounted on the roof, collects sunlight on stationary mirrors which reflect it through high, narrow windows on the first floor. Another series of mirrors then transmits this light to the target zone—an east/west strip that cuts across the upper region of the lab. Surprisingly, even on a gloomy day, a fair amount of daylight is reflected inside. The cheap, abundant sunlight provided by the system is 50 percent cooler than the light that comes from a fluorescent source. Supplementary lighting in the lab is provided by fluorescent luminaires.

The environmental and mineral laboratories and offices, and the Underground Space Center, are set up in an area mined out of sandstone 30 feet below a layer of limestone. The 2-storey lab center has a naturally constant, stable temperature of 55 degrees and is vibration-free. The labs and offices are completely insulated from the area's drastic swings in temperature—from 100° heat in the summer to subzero temperatures in winter.
An active solar system brings daylight to this insulated level far underground. Equipment for the solar system is housed in an above-ground cupola. Clock-driven mirrors are steered to constantly face the sun. The tracking is controlled with the use of a Hewlett Packard programmable calculator. The sunlight collected by the mirrors

is concentrated and directed down through a shaft via a series of lenses and mirrors. The sunlight emerges through a glass ceiling panel to illuminate an office seven stories below. The architect believes that in the future the active system may perhaps be designed to operate at night with an intense electric source—a xenon arc lamp, for example—for a fraction of what it would cost to use a standard fluorescent system.

A few feet from the shaft is an Ectascope. It is a simulated window, much like a television screen, that offers a view of a lecture hall above ground, surrounded by lawn and trees. It operates like a periscope to provide the underground inhabitants with a link to the above-ground world.

Conventional fluorescent and incandescent lighting is used everywhere else in the building. The interiors are designed intentionally to look subdued and unremarkable, because the architect believes people feel most comfortable in low-key, familiar surroundings. The color scheme consists of warm, earth tones—rust-red, tan and beige.

A second portion of the building visible above ground is a clerestory-banded rotunda that serves as a visual focal point. The room is ringed with columns on center at the doorways.

Classrooms are located on the west side of the building and are accessible to the School of Architecture. The classrooms are shadowed purposely by the Space Science Center because light control is needed for frequent audio-visual presentations.

Faculty offices have a southern exposure and are stepped down into a sunken courtyard. In addition to the solar optics located on the building's north side, a water-filled Trombe wall (a hybrid solar heating system) is positioned on the south side.

The Civil and Mineral Engineering Building is a prime and successful example of totally custom-designed architecture and engineering.

A number of passive solar energy systems are incorporated into the five percent of the building which projects above ground: supplementary heating with a trombe wall system, solar shading and wind control with plant material and a unique system for optically projecting sunlight and exterior views into deep interior space. A parallel active solar energy design system provides supplementary heating, cooling and electrification in tandem with the passive systems.

Gateway to seven buildings to the south which comprise the university's Institute of Technology.

Longitudinal section.

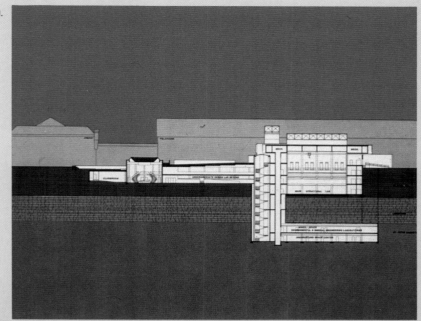

A vertical slice through the building.

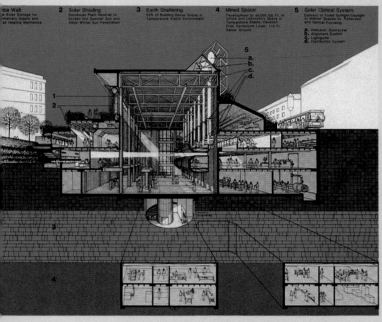

A spiraling plaza leads to an underground pedestrian system that links neighboring buildings and a bus transit corridor along the north edge of the site.

The above-ground portion of the main structural lab is 50 feet high.

Rotunda banded by clerestory. All spaces except the rotunda and classrooms are attached to the main structural lab.

Passive solar optic system includes a fresnel lens on
the right and a north sky monitor on the left that
provide light to the main structural lab.

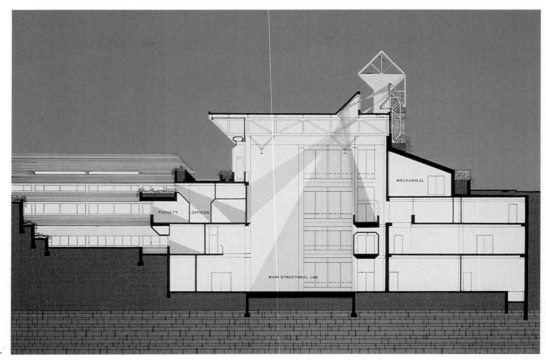

Passive solar lighting.

Fluorescent lighting at the top pedestrian walkway supplements the passive solar system.

The sunlight is collected by a monitor and reflected by mirrors to the target zone—an east-west swatch of the main structural lab.

Above-ground cupola in which the sun is tracked by
mirrors.

Sunlight is collected, concentrated and relayed by mirrors and lenses down a shaft.

Active solar lighting and periscope system diagram.

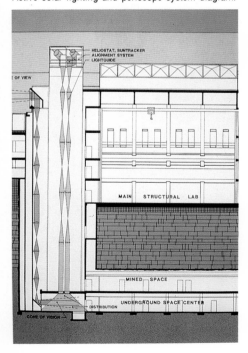

A view from the periscope, seven floors below ground, to a part of the campus above ground.

The Statue of Liberty

Lighting Designers: Howard Brandston, Principal; Gene Stival, Associate-in-Charge; Chou Lien, Associate—Production: Thomas Thompson, Markus Earley, Alexander Radunsky, Daniel Lotten and S. Kelly Shannon; Howard Brandston Lighting Design, Inc., New York, NY
(Special thanks to the General Electric Co.: Ralph Ketchum, Peter Von Hermann, Dr. Gilbert Reiling, Mary Beth Gotti, and Ron Paugh)

Sculptor: Frederic Auguste Bartholdi

Original Structural Engineer: Gustave Eiffel

Restoration Architect: Swanke Hayden Connell

Restoration Mechanical, Structural and Electrical Engineer: Annan & Whitney Engineers

Client: National Parks Service

Project Location: New York, NY

Preparations for the Statue of Liberty's new lighting design began as early as November, 1983, when the designer commenced visits to the monument for study before the scaffolding was erected. All possible locations for the lighting equipment were established and measurements of distance and angle were recorded. Photographs of the Statue were taken from every viewing angle—bridges, highways, promenades, the harbor.

The rationale chosen for the design by the lighting consultant is twofold:

1. The beauty of the architectural details would be enhanced best by recreating at night qualities of daylight and its effects on the monument.

2. The illumination should enforce an aura of dignity appropriate for a national symbol of freedom and homeland and should not be overly dramatic or glaring.

To accomplish the first objective, light sources were needed which would mimic the natural interplay of light and shadow and the color rendering of sunlight. Two light sources were sought—one which would render "warmly" the prominent surfaces of the Statue; another which would render "cooly" the soft, shadowed folds and nooks.

All existing light sources were tested, and it was found that they rendered the green patina of the Statue either too dramatic, or too muddy. Consequently, the designer worked with a team of scientists and researchers from the manufacturer to devise two new 250-watt metal halide lamps: a "cool" source, rated at 5200 degrees Kelvin, and a "warm" one, near 3800 degrees Kelvin. Each lamp has an initial light output of 20,000 lumens. Life expectancy is two to three years, and it is recommended the lamps be replaced as a group. It is expected that the color rendering will remain constant throughout the life of the lamps.

The second objective—to create a majestic, yet welcoming presence in the harbor—is embodied in the gradual brightening and intensifying of illumination from the base to the crown. This darker-to-brighter approach pulls the eye upward and emphasizes the height of the Statue.

The latest technology was applied to reach the gradation and blending of color, light and shadow on the sculpted surfaces of the Statue. Computer simulations, showing different colors projected onto the Statue at a variety of angles and equipment locations were made and compared with on-the-spot testing. The optimum combination was translated into reality with the aid of carefully designed fixtures.

Precise control of the beams from the luminaires eliminates spill light. The double-polished high-purity aluminum reflector can project a high-intensity narrow beam of over one million candlepower. A thin glass coating protects the reflector from dulling and losing efficiency. The beams are very specifically focused—on a hand, the outer edge of the book, the inside of a fold.

The small island on which the monument rests is swept by strong winds that carry industrial and urban pollution. In conventional luminaires, circulating air deposits particles of dirt on the optical surface. In the new units, a charcoal filter is included that purifies the air entering the fixture. The luminaires meet the National Park Administration's requirements for trouble-free, low-cost maintenance. Forty metal halide fixtures positioned in five ground-level pits around the island's edge illuminate the body of the Statue.

The torch and crown at the top are highlighted with additional, special illumination. The original torch was composed of yellow cathedral glass held together by an iron frame and illuminated from within. Before it was removed and placed on view in the museum inside the base of the Statue, portions of the original torch were covered with gold foil, so experiments with light sources could be conducted.

The new torch held aloft is covered with gold leaf and illuminated from without by two types of lamps. Sixteen 250-watt tungsten halogen PAR lamps are mounted under the railings of the torch base, and 42 120-watt, 6-volt very narrow spot lamps (like those used to monitor clarity of air on airport runways) are positioned on ground level.

The crown, and the visitor's area within it, were illuminated originally by an industrial fixture. A copy of it was made from brass, based on its appearance in old photographs, and installed inside the crown. To highlight the view of the crown from the outside, four 1000-watt PAR-64 medium flood lamps are mounted inside the back of the head and direct light out through the viewing windows in the crown.

The visitor traffic circulation system has been redesigned. Stairs and elevators take visitors to the double helical stairs that lead to the windows that look out onto the harbor. The gradual-brightening technique used on the exterior was carried into the interior of the Statue. The journey up to the crown begins at the dimly-lit entry area. As the visitor ascends, each level becomes brighter until daylight floods the observation area in the crown. Along the way, structural features—beams, joints, bolts—are highlighted to encourage appreciation of the craftsmanship. The interior of the Statue is lighted with currently available incandescent and fluorescent luminaires, except for some specially built fixtures and mounting devices.

Through illumination, Lady Liberty has become a nighttime beacon in the harbor, not garish or glaring, but a majestic symbol of freedom and homeland, maintaining its own presence against the backdrop of glittering skyscrapers.

The lighting gradually becomes brighter from the base to the top,
where the gold-leaf covered torch brilliantly reflects the light.

Computer modelling was used in all phases of the lighting design, including lamp and reflector development.

"Liberty Englightening the World" is the formal name of the 151-foot statue. The night lighting duplicates the visual effects of daylight on the statue.

CHAPTER 8 NEW PRODUCTS

The sampling of new products which follows is not intended to be a comprehensive collection of all that is new in the lighting marketplace. Only companies contacted which submitted the requested materials within the specified time frame are included.

Three concepts can be used to describe current trends in the lighting industry: refinement, flexibility and specialization.

Refinement

There is an emphasis today on refining existing sources and fixtures to increase energy efficiency, performance and cost savings. Methods used most to achieve this include:

■ Increasing beam control and eliminating spill light through techniques such as silvering the tops of high-intensity discharge (HID) sources and developing more sophisticated reflector designs.

■ Improving color rendering of HID sources, particularly high-pressure sodium (HPS) and metal halide, so that they will correspond more closely to incandescent rendering.

In an attempt to encourage replacement of incandescent lamps with the more efficient HID and fluorescent lamps, manufacturers have developed the following:

■ Miniaturized HID and fluorescent sources. Both lamps and

housings are becoming less bulky, and more compact and attractive.

■ Compact adapters for sources requiring ballasts that can be screwed directly into incandescent sockets. This enables the designer to specify more energy-efficient sources in areas, such as corridors, where color is not critical and where incandescent lighting would probably have been used in the past.

■ Improved sensors that make it possible for lights to be switched off automatically when not in use. Also, the use of dimming controls, which extend lamp life and save energy, has become more widespread.

Flexibility

The refinements mentioned above, as well as others, have resulted in increased flexibility in the application of sources and fixtures. Other developments which have increased the variety of equipment available and the flexibility in its use include:

■ An emphasis on aesthetics. Lighting products today are not only expected to perform well, but to look good, too. Today there are more architectural and decorative fixtures and accessories in a greater variety of shapes, sizes and colors than ever before.

■ The use of computers, which enables the designer to spend less time on calculations and to visualize a space by displaying brightness levels and layout before the installation is constructed. The computer age can result in more custom-designed, less standardized environments in the future, a better suiting of means to client needs, and increased long-range energy and cost savings.

Specialization

In recent years, there has been a profusion of small lighting manufacturers that specialize in one or two product lines or areas—for example, recessed and track fixtures, or adaptors, or outdoor HID lamps. Large companies have a tendency to focus on a mass marketplace and produce a large volume per product. Being set up for large volume production inhibits the capacity for quick or constant change. Lower-volume manufacturers have the freedom to experiment and custom-design more frequently.

Larger companies eventually will selectively choose and mass produce products introduced by smaller manufacturers, after the innovations have become commonplace and demand has increased significantly. But in the meantime, because of the increase in small innovation-oriented companies, the range of products available and the speed with which changes in equipment occur will most likely increase.

Alkco

Varilux™ three-level task light integrates two lamps (13-watt PL fluorescent) into a single luminaire. A specially-designed reflector and lens direct light laterally from the sides and across the workstation to minimize glare, veiling reflections and shadows. A recessed retainer hides chords. The fixture is easily mounted to the underside of metal shelves without tools, using a quick-install mounting bracket, with double-faced adhesive strips.

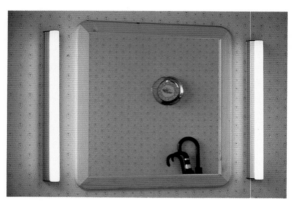

Lincandescents™, which are available in 12-, 20- and 40-inch lengths, add strokes of incandescent warmth to both commercial and residential settings. Several can be placed in repeated patterns for longer runs. The fixtures are finished in gold, silver or black, with etched or hand-polished specular surfaces. Attractive triangular side reflectors can be added to make a variety of design statements, while covering unsightly electrical boxes. The continuous 45-degree beveled platform emphasizes the source's streamlined form.

Architectural Lighting Systems Inc.

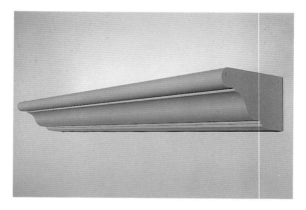

The cove lighting system is a wall-mounted indirect light source that reflects the contemporary attitude towards architectural detail. It is available in four decorative styles and various lengths. It received the 1987 Corporate Design & Realty Citation Award.

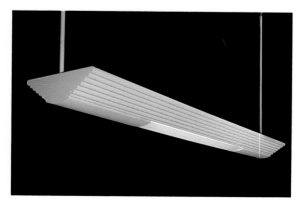

This indirect/direct luminaire is available in four decorative styles and over 950 colors.

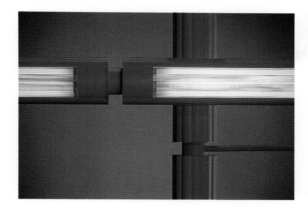

The one-lamp direct fluorescent linear system is available in three decorative styles and various standard and custom lengths.

Shown are several of the indirect/direct, task, cove, indirect and valance luminaires available in over 950 colors.

Arte De Mexico

The wood and iron chandelier (C-545) is 25 inches high and 35 inches in diameter.

The wall-mounted fixture (W-185) measures 18 inches high, 12 inches wide and 6 inches in diameter.

Arte De Mexico

The wall-mounted fixture (W-100) is 26 inches high, 17 inches wide and 16 inches in diameter.

Atelier International Lighting

Murana, designed by Perry A. King and Santiago Miranda for Arteluce, has a formed-steel backplate that supports an aluminum stem. Diffusors in blue, light gray or white, with reflective white backgrounds, are constructed of opal glass inner panels, bonded to silk-screened glass outer panels. Two opaque blue or white triangular-shaped end caps with combination textured and high-gloss surfaces hold the glass panels securely in place. A 135-watt clear incandescent bulb provides illumination.

Tikal was designed by Italian architect, Pier Giuseppe Ramella. The glass structure (19 inches wide by 17.7 inches high) is clear blue, sand-blasted on one side, polished on the other. Diffusers are opal white and gray injection-molded methacrylate. The weighted metal base, finished in anthracite-gray enamel, rotates 330 degrees, permitting the user to choose which light intensity should face outward.

Club was designed by Pier Giuseppe Ramella for Arteluce. The conical-shaped metal base stands 35 inches high. Its translucent thermoplastic lamphead and a frosted acrylic diffuser each rotate 330 degrees. A height-adjustable arm, with a molded rubber handgrip at the top of the base, can be vertically extended up to 11 inches. The light source is a 20-watt halogen lamp. Color choices include lamphead and arm in red with an anthracite gray enamel base or lamphead and arm in black with a white base.

Ciao, designed by architect Ezio Didone for Arteluce, is made up of an octagon-shaped, extruded aluminum base 5 inches wide, 5½ inches long and 3 inches high. It stands on two track-like feet and provides the platform for a flexible steel tube neck containing the lamphead and a 20-watt halogen light source. The neck permits the lamphead to be positioned in any direction for direct or reflected light at differing heights. The lamphead itself rotates 330 degrees and the base can be wall mounted. Color choices include white or red enamelled base, with black plastic end caps and black plastic caps on the feet, or matte black enamelled aluminum base with black end caps and red plastic caps on the feet.

Triana, designed by Perry A. King and Santiago Miranda for Arteluce, has a die-cast aluminum weighted base supporting an aluminum stem. Diffusors consist of opal glass inner panels, bonded to silk-screened glass outer panels, in blue, light gray or white, each with reflective white backgrounds. Two opaque blue or white triangular-shaped end caps with combination textured and high-gloss surfaces hold the glass panels securely in place. A 300-watt tungsten-halogen light source is used.

Onda, designed by Ezio Didone for Arteluce, is available with an A-19 100-watt bulb. The 15-inch round, 6½-inch high, U.L.-listed lamp is characterized by a series of concentric circular grooves in an opalescent cone-shaped plexiglass diffuser, set into its red, white or black enamelled steel housing. Onda fits closely to wall or ceiling to provide an even distribution of light that facilitates mounting individually or in clusters.

Palio, designed by Perry A. King and Santiago Miranda, stands 15.7 inches high and 13.8 inches wide. It illuminates through an elliptical, two-piece, opal glass diffuser body and from a crescent-shaped aluminum reflector suspended by thin chrome-plated brass rods over the diffuser. A black die-cast aluminum base incorporates a full range rotary dimmer on/off switch. Palio's reflector is available in polished aluminum or polished copper-plated finishes, with a textured matte-white inner surface.

The Bodine Company

The HID 1600 emergency lighting system utilizes high intensity discharge lamps for both normal AC and emergency lighting. The system does not affect normal operation or lamp life, and there is no need for quartz restrike and auxiliary emergency lighting. The two major components of the system are a DC power supply and remote ballasts. Power to lamps is never interrupted because the batteries continuously "float" on a DC circuit at a slightly lower voltage level. If AC power fails or drops, current automatically flows from the battery to operate the lamps until power is restored.

Shown are the remote inverter ballast (left) and DC power supply of the HID 1600 emergency lighting system. Each remote ballast contains its own inverter and is installed at the fixture, eliminating the need for AC ballasts. The DC power supply, battery charger, rectifier/filter and controls are contained in a cabinet which should be installed in an equipment room or similar area.

Brilliant Lighting Inc.

The Halo Swing is a 35-watt halogen desk lamp with a swivel arm and rotating head, available in black, white, red or yellow.

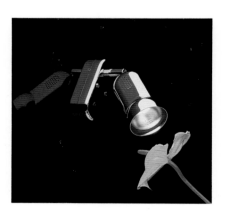

The Laser 63 Deluxe gold-plated spotlight can be used as a wall or shelf light. The on/off switch is located on the base plate. It is also available in portable tracks (two on a 20-inch bar, or three on a 40-inch bar) and as a ceiling fixture (three on a round plate).

D'Lights

The new wall sconce, designed and released exclusively by D'Lights, is available in rose, bottle green, champagne and clear, with either a chrome or brass cap. The diffusion of light is caused by the crystal clear prismatic glass.

Eastrock Technology, Inc.

The small (less than 2 inches in diameter), efficient Compact U™ Adapter uses a toroidal ballast that consumes less than 2 watts, operates the lamp efficiently and quietly with low operating temperatures. The FUL Type lamps are constructed of heavy gauge, 15 millimeter diameter glass and institutional quality components. These provide extended life (9,000 hours) and a very warm fluorescent color tone that closely matches the color of incandescent bulbs.

Direct Wire Adapters allow for both initial and replacement applications where permanent wiring is required. They share the features of the company's standard screw-in units. The connecting wires can be positioned from either side or from the bottom, or an IPS threaded connector can be attached for final installation.

The Shoehorn Adapter revolves on the brass ratchet socket to allow exact directional light output. The highly polished, reflective surface increases light produced by the lamps. The reflector is permanently attached to the adapter, but can be tilted up to 15 degrees. The company's standard toroidal ballast is used.

Eastrock
Technology, Inc.

The High-Pressure Sodium Adapter allows the retrofit of existing costly incandescent sockets with energy-efficient high-pressure sodium lamps by simply screwing the adapter into the socket. There is no need for rewiring or refixturing. It is also available in direct wire.

The Halogen Adapter features a replaceable 2,000-hour halogen lamp that operates cooly on normal current (110/120 volts). The toroidal ballast consumes less than 2 watts. The adapter is available in 5 watts and 10 watts, and in two designs (flood and spot). The adapters are small enough (under 2 inches in diameter) to install easily in track lighting, display cases, trade show displays, mannequin ensembles or window display areas.

The Quad Adapter allows for a 33 percent reduction in overall height compared to a normal compact fluorescent. The adapter operates all brands of 9 watt and 13 watt compact fluorescent quad lamps within manufacturers' specifications. It features a small diameter, high efficiency and low wattage consumption. Reflector covers are available for more downlight.

The Threaded Cap Adapter has a universally threaded, solid aluminum (.04 gauge) cap. The company's standard screw-in adapter is permanently attached to the cap. The cap design allows free flow of air, while still being water-tight. It is available in two heights based on the wattage lamp desired, with either prismatic acrylic or prismatic polycarbonate lens.

Reflectorized compact fluorescents are constructed of polished spun aluminum with a two-layer enamel finish. The combination of a photometrically designed reflector and the mirror-like finish, accelerate and drive the light far in excess of the lamp's standard lumen rating. They are available in five sizes and two lens arrangements.

Enercon
Data
Corporation

The Fashion Plates come in four basic colors (gold, bronze, pewter and silver). Additional colors can be custom ordered. The plates are brushed, anodized aluminum of .040 thickness and have black rocker switches and matching black screws. There are three standard configurations: single gang, one switch; single gang, 2 switch; and double gang, 4 switch. Other configurations can be custom ordered. The switches are designed to control Enercon's low-voltage transformer/relay.

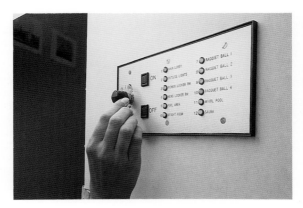

The Rotary Switch Panel allows for control of up to 144 transformer relays and provides for up to 12 control zones. Each of the 12 control zones can be either a single transformer relay or it can control up to 12 transformer relays in a group. Twelve green lights indicate the on/off status of each zone, with space for up to 15 engraved characters to identify each zone. A locator light illuminates the rotary switch. The face plate is of brushed aluminum on a black frame.

Feldman
Lighting

Traditional (#8146) is a nine-lamp chandelier with polished brass, 26½ inches wide and 22 inches high.

Feldman
Lighting

Art Deco (#4056) is a four-lamp chandelier with polished brass, 22 inches wide, 12 inches high and 31 inches O.A.L.

General
Electric
Lighting
Business
Group

The coated Halarc™ 32-watt metal halide lamp has an initial light output of 2,500 lm and a rated median life of 7,500 hours at 11 hours per start. The lamp's color temperature is 3000 Kelvin with a color-rendering index of 65. The Halarc operates in a vertical, base-up mode and requires no fixture enclosure, making it an excellent source for downlighting luminaires, and a good replacement for incandescent lighting in corridors, lobbies, entrances and meeting rooms. The single-lamp electronic ballast, in a case resembling a fluorescent ballast, fastens easily across the mounting brackets of a typical downlighting fixture. The Halarc lamp is for use on 277-volt wiring systems.

Holophane

The ParkLane™ area luminaire features a light control design incorporating a rear-surface metallized, prismatic glass reflector. The optical elements allow a choice of square or offset rectangular light patterns without the need for refractors or an inordinately large number of fixtures. The optical system is enclosed in a one-piece, integrated prismatic cube/cone constructed of seamless acrylic. Housing above the cube is of extruded aluminum. The luminaire can be wall mounted, top or side pole mounted individually or in multiple arrangements. It can accommodate mercury, metal halide or high-pressure sodium lamps from 200 watts to 400 watts.

The GranVille™ outdoor luminaire contains a prismatic refractor that helps direct light into an efficient, rectangular pattern, permitting long spacings with excellent uniformity. The luminaires are available with either low wattage high-pressure sodium, mercury or metal halide lamps. In retrofit projects, they are highly compatible with other existing poles.

Juno
Lighting, Inc.

These four low-voltage trac spotlights (Notch Back™, Open Back, Notch Back™ Pendant and Cube) can be used with either Juno Power Pack (50V A-12 V coil and core, or 75V A-12 V solid-state electronic transformer). They are designed around the MR16 lamp, which produces a precise light beam and good color rendition. A variety of finishes, color filters and accessories are available.

The miniature Notch-Back™ (T443) made of die-cast aluminum, measures 2½ inches long and 2½ inches in diameter with a 1⅝-inch aperture.

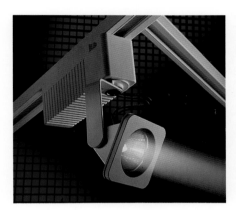

The Open Back (T440) measures 2¼ inches long and 2½ inches square with a 1⅝-inch aperture. The fixture's face plate and pivot mount are made of die-cast aluminum.

The Cube (T441) measures 3¼ inches long and 2½ inches square with a 1⅝-inch aperture. The housing is constructed of seamless steel; the bezel of die-cast aluminum.

The Notch Back™ Pendant (TP433) is made of die-cast aluminum and can be positioned at any point along its 13½-inch metal rod. It measures 2½ inches long and 2½ inches in diameter with a 1⅝-inch aperture.

Juno
Lighting, Inc.

The Open Yoke track spotlight (T444) measures 3⅞ inches long and 5 inches in diameter with a 4-inch aperture. The lampholder rotates 358 degrees horizontally and 105 degrees vertically. It is designed around the 12-V PAR36 lamp and incorporates a Juno 50-volt A coil and core Power Pack transformer (T531). The Open Yoke is ideal for interiors where longer throws of light are needed. White or black finish is available.

The PAR38 Open Yoke track light (T368) measures 5¾ inches long and 5 inches in diameter with a 4½ inch aperture. It can be used on either a one- or two-circuit track. The lampholder is designed for use with a medium-base PAR38 lamp. The precisely controlled beam spreads make it an excellent choice for highlighting merchandise displays, lobbies and interiors.

Koch + Lowy

Footsteps (F-3005), designed by Charles Keller, stands 74 inches high with an 11-inch diameter shade. The feet and shade are covered with a suede-like, nonreflective finish that is scratch resistant. The feet are gray. Shade/leg color combinations are: black/yellow, black/black, polished brass/yellow, and polished chrome/black. The lamp uses a 500-watt halogen bulb and has a full range dimmer.

Flip, designed by De Majo, is available in wall-mount (P-54, W-54) and standing (F-5004) models. The glass is 7 inches in diameter and 5 inches high. The wall-mount model has a 5-inch diameter backplate and a 9-inch extension. The standing model is 72 inches high with a 13-inch diameter base. The glass is available in white with clear reveal or burgundy with orange reveal. Hardware is black or white. A 25-watt double envelope halogen bulb is included in both models. Wall-mounts come with a hi-low switch on the backplate (P-54), or with no switch (W-54).

Nottingham (T-500), designed by Antony Howard, is 12 inches high, with a 10½-inch diameter shade and 4-inch base. The shade and base are gray and are covered with a suede-like, nonreflective finish that is scratch resistant. The stem and finial are available in polished brass, chrome, red and yellow. The lamp uses a 13-watt PL fluorescent bulb.

LAM Lighting Systems

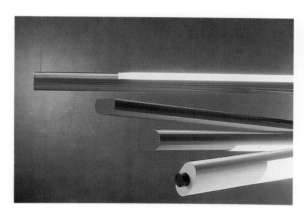

ELAN™ lighting systems are oval-shaped extruded aluminum, linear, fluorescent accent and ambient lighting elements. They are available in direct, indirect and directable configurations using lenses and diffusers. ELAN comes in straight runs and patterns, is lit by Octron or rapid-start lamps and is easily mounted.

Lighting Systems Inc.

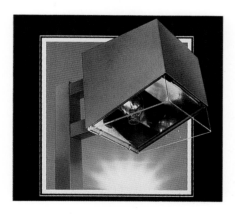

The Sunburst Series of outdoor luminaires is designed to utilize high-pressure sodium, super metal halide, metal halide and deluxe mercury vapor lamps. The one-piece aluminum housing is available in dark bronze, black, white or sandstone baked-on powdered polyester. Other colors are available on request. The Sunburst features a sharp backside cutoff which eliminates spill light. An IES Type IV distribution reflector is used.

The Cypress Series outdoor fixtures are made for use with low-pressure sodium lamps. Its optical system allows diversity with two lighting distribution patterns. The one-piece formed reflector is the standard of the series and offers IES Type II distribution. For general area lighting, an IES Type III distribution is available. This reflector system creates a high-performance, uniform pattern. The standard finish of the steel luminaires is primed. Bronze, black, sandstone or white finishes are optional.

Lightscape, Inc.

Nastro (32202/7) from Stilnovo uses a 50-watt, 12-volt halogen light source.

Leggio (31401/2) from Stilnovo uses a 500-watt halogen light source.

Palomar (29021/2/5) from Stilnovo uses a 500-watt halogen light source.

Zagar (24041/2/5) from Stilnovo uses a 500-watt halogen light source.

Bascula (29011/3) from Stilnovo uses a 150-watt halogen light source.

Samurai (12021/2/3) from Stilnovo uses a 300-watt halogen light source.

Maniglia (32022) from Stilnovo uses a 50-watt, 12-volt halogen light source.

Flu designed by Giusto Toso. Sconce by Barovier & Toso.

Lightscape, Inc.

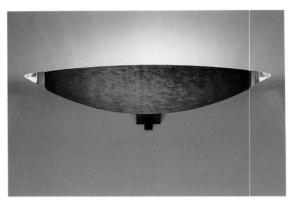

Fuochi Artificiali ("Fireworks"), designed by Angelo Barovier. Triangular chandelier by Barovier & Toso.

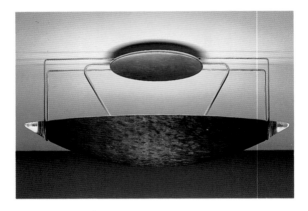

Fuochi Artificiali ("Fireworks") designed by Angelo Barovier. Sconce by Barovier & Toso.

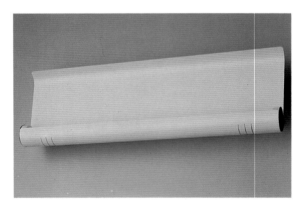

Shell (49021) from Stilnovo uses a 20-watt fluorescent tube.

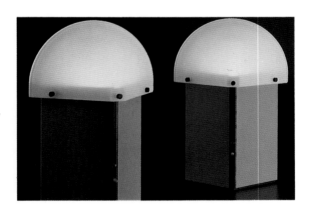

Pinguina (18041) from Stilnovo uses a 60-watt incandescent light source.

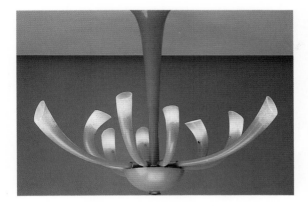

Flu designed by Giusto Toso. Ceiling mount by Barovier & Toso.

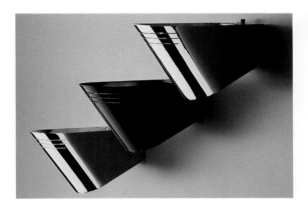

Prua (26020/1/2/8) from Stilnovo uses a 150-watt halogen light source.

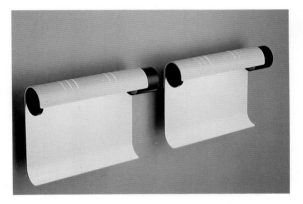

Shell (49001) uses an 11-watt PL , and model 49011 operates with a 150 W halogen light source. Both are from Stilnovo.

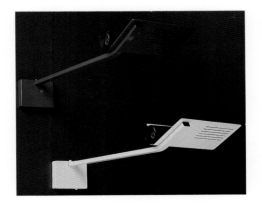

Leggio (31501/2) uses a 500-watt halogen light source.

Lightscape, Inc.

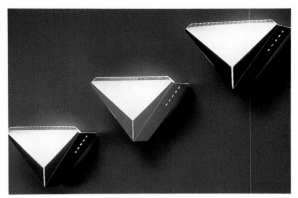

Palma (19020/1/2/3/7/8) from Stilnovo uses a 100-watt incandescent light source.

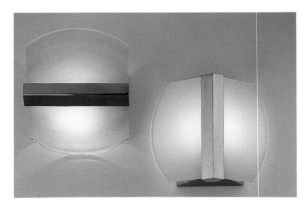

Sera designed by Rudi Dordoni. Sconce and ceiling mount by Barovier & Toso.

Lutron Electronics Co., Inc.

The front surface of Nova T* Thin Profile Lighting Control projects just over 1/4 inch from the wall. Its new thin design still maintains the features of the original Nova line, including: linear slide control for easy, precise adjustment of lighting level; high capacity up to 1500 watts; voltage compensation; and maximum RFI filtering. A variety of colors, finishes, and faceplate options are available to complement any interior design. White is the standard color with beige, gray, brown, and black also available from stock. One-piece multi-gang faceplates (optional) provide an attractive, seamless appearance for ganged installation.

OptiFlure™, the small area fluorescent dimming system, works with standard fluorescent ballasts and lamps and uses existing wiring. The system consists of a lighting controller (shown) and a wallbox slide control. A single wallbox control can operate up to 10 lighting controllers. A preset rocker switch allows on/off control without disturbing the light level setting on the slider. Dimming can be achieved from 100 percent to 25 percent light. Proper filament voltage is maintained for full lamp life.

Mary Street Studio

Available in matte gray, theLight is a combined copyholder and task light specially designed for use at computer terminals. It stands approximately 13 inches high and 10 inches wide and uses a 40T10 incandescent lamp. It has received IBD and Roscoe awards.

Mitsubishi Electric Sales America, Inc.

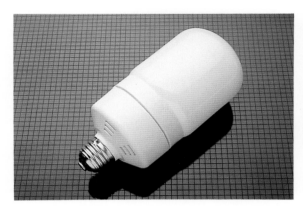

The Marathon fluorescent light bulbs can be used interchangeably with, or as direct replacements for, incandescent bulbs used in home and industry. The 10 models of Marathon bulbs are offered in either globe or cylindrical shapes, at 15 watts or 13 watts, in clear or opaque. The bulb is available in two colors: warm white (similar to incandescent) and a studio light version (the best known sunlight purity for true color rendition). The energy-efficient 15-watt bulb is the equivalent of a 60- or 65-watt incandescent bulb in light output. Life expectancy is 9,000 hours.

The Marathon Torch, a Marathon bulb and light fixture combination, can be placed conveniently on a table or desk top, or wall mounted. It is available in a red, beige, brass or wood grain finish.

NL Corporation

One of a line of recessed fixtures for General Electric's 32-watt Halarc™ metal halide lamp. Fixtures have an electronic ballast, are available in 120 volts and 277 volts and are damp location listed as standard.

Ron Rezek
Lighting
+ Furniture

Ovuli has an anodized aluminum base topped with an etched glass dome. It measures 23 inches by 16 inches in diameter, operates with a 100-watt, G-40 lamp, and includes 6 feet of cord. The base is available in red and blue, or all black.

The stem of Iris contains a touch-operated switch that controls three levels of halogen light. Standard colors include: Base—black wrinkle finish; Pole—flat black, light gray, or polished nickel; Shade—gloss black, white, pink, or blue-green. Marble bases and special finishes are available. Iris measures 74 inches high with a 6-inch shade and 10-inch base. One 250-watt quartz halogen lamp and 6 feet of black cord are included.

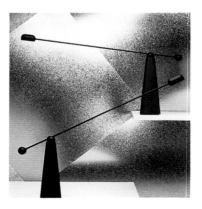

Orbis is 13 inches high with a 32-inch span. The ball joint that tops the pedestal rotates 360 degrees horizontally and 30 degrees vertically. Orbis is available in all flat black or flat black with a red stem. A 50-watt incandescent bulb and 6 feet of black cord are included.

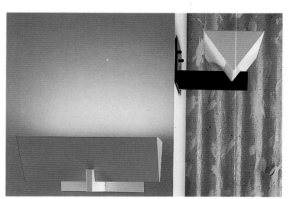

The Kavanaugh Sconce, designed by Gene Kavanaugh, is a triangular shade supported by an arm that leaves the line of the wall unbroken. Stock finish: arm in white or satin black; shade in white. Other standard and custom colors are available on the shade. It measures 12 inches wide, 5 inches high and 9 inches deep. Double socket incandescent, single 13-watt fluorescent, or halogen lamps can be used.

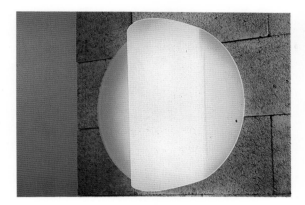

The Cymbal, a convolution of a circle, is a simple glass disc glowing with a slight green tint. It measures 17 inches in diameter and 5½ inches deep and is available with either two standard incandescent bulbs or two PL-13 fluorescents.

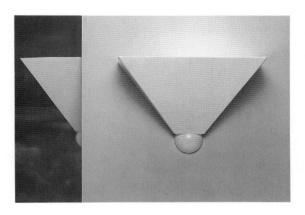

Arno is available in incandescent, fluorescent or halogen versions and in a variety of finishes, including gold or silver leaf. Stock finish: pebble white. It measures 9 inches high, 14 inches wide and 6 inches deep.

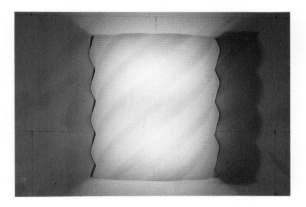

Scroll is molded ½-inch glass formed in an elegant shape with top and bottom open. It glows with a subtle green tint and is available with standard-incandescent or 28-watt fluorescent lamping. It is 15 inches tall, 12 inches wide and 6 inches deep.

Tishman Research Company

Infracon[R], mounted in the ceiling or on the wall and wired into the lighting system, operates by sensing and responding to the presence of infrared heat given off naturally by the human body as it moves. It turns lights on when people enter an office and off when they leave, maximizing the efficient use of energy.

AWARDS INFORMATION

Albert S. Bard Awards for Excellence in Architecture and Urban Design

The Bard Award was established in 1963 by the City Club of New York, a leading civic organization. Although originally awarded to honor civic architecture, today any project built in New York City is eligible. Ada Louise Huxtable has called the Bard Awards "a barometer for the architecture of this nation."

The awards are named after the late Albert S. Bard, former trustee of the City Club of New York, who for 60 years fought vigorously for a better city. The jury, many of whom are outstanding professionals in the architectural community, is independent of the City Club. For more information, contact:

> The City Club of New York
> 33 West 42 Street
> New York, NY 10036

Edison Award

The Edison Award competition is open to lighting professionals who employ significant use of any General Electric lamps in a lighting design project. While the lighting installation need not be achieved exclusively through the use of General Electric lamps, the entry will be judged on the degree of achievement of certain criteria through significant use of GE lamp products.

The first prize is a customized Steuben crystal creation personalized with the winner's name. A distinctive plaque is presented to the owner of the installation. Similar plaques are awarded to entries reaching the final judging stage.

Entries will be judged on: functional excellence; architectural compatibility; effective use of state-of-the-art lighting products and techniques; good color, form and texture revelation; and energy and cost effectiveness. The panel of five judges represents the American Institute of Architects, the American Society of Interior Designers, the International Association of Lighting Designers, the Illuminating Engineering Society of North America, and the General Electric Company.

The competition was established in 1983. A descriptive brochure and entry form may be obtained by writing:

> Edison Award Competition
> General Electric Company
> Nela Park # 4162
> Cleveland, OH   44112

Halo/SPI National Lighting Competition

The competition is sponsored by Halo Lighting and held under the auspices of the American Society of Interior Designers. It was established in 1977 to honor designers who excel in the creative use of lighting as a basic element of design. Originality and technical ability are judged in designs using Halo Lighting Power-Trac track lighting, downlighting and SPI ambient/task indirect lighting.

Several awards are usually granted every year in each of two categories: First Place and Honorable Mention. Contact:

Halo Lighting
400 Busse Road
Elk Grove Village, IL 60007

International Illumination Design Awards Program

The Program, which is not a competition, provides an opportunity for public recognition of professionalism, ingenuity, and originality of lighting design based upon the individual merit of each entry judged against specific criteria. Criteria include considerations such as the complexity of the design problems and solutions and how well they deal with energy effectiveness, environmental limitations, costs, originality, and suitability for and consistency with aesthetic and functional requirements.

Judges are selected from a broad professional spectrum which represents knowledge of lighting and design excellence. The awards are presented on several levels, beginning with local and regional. The highest honors include the Edwin F. Guth Memorial Special Citation, Award of Excellence and Award of Distinction. The Excellence and Distinction awards consist of one glass sculpture per design team, and one plaque per owner. All other awards are certificates. For further information, contact:

Illuminating Engineering Society of North America
345 East 47th Street
New York, NY 10017

Lighting Design Awards Program

The Awards Program was begun in 1983 to increase awareness of good lighting design. Projects must demonstrate aesthetic achievement, technical merit, and sensitivity to the architectural concept. Certificates are presented for Awards of Excellence, and Honorable Mentions. Nonmembers as well as members of the International Association of Lighting Designers may enter. For more information, write:

International Association of Lighting Designers
18 East 16th Street, Suite 208
New York, NY 10003

INDEX 1
LIGHTING DESIGNERS

INDEX 2
LIGHTING DESIGN FIRMS

INDEX 3
DESIGNERS/ DESIGN FIRMS

INDEX 4
ARCHITECTS/ARCHITECTURAL FIRMS

INDEX 5
ENGINEERS/ ENGINEERING FIRMS

INDEX 6
PHOTOGRAPHERS

INDEX 7
CLIENTS